Unmasking Evil

———◆———

The Serial Killer Encyclopedia, Healthcare Edition — Nurses and Doctors Who Kill

Jonny Cassidy

© Copyright 2023 Jonny Cassidy – ALL rights reserved,

The contents of the book may not be reproduced, duplicated or transmitted without the direct written permission from the publisher or author.

Under no circumstances will any legal responsibility or blame be held against the publisher or author for any reparation, damages, or monetary loss due to the information herein, either directly or indirectly.

Legal Notice:

This book is copyright protected. This is only for personal use. You cannot amend, distribute, sell, use, quote or paraphrase any part or the content within this book without the consent of the author or publisher.

Disclaimer Notice:

Please note the information contained within this document is for educational and entertainment purposes only. Every attempt has been made to provide accurate, up-to-date and reliable information. No warranties of any kind are expressed or implied. Readers acknowledge that the author is not engaging in rendering legal, financial, medical or professional advice. The content of this book has been derived from various sources. Please consult a licensed professional before attempting any techniques outlined in this book.

By reading this document, the reader agrees that under no circumstances is the author or publisher responsible for any losses, direct or indirect, which are incurred as a result of the use of the information contained within this document, including but not limited to, --errors and omissions, or inaccuracies.

Table of Contents

Introduction	1
Chapter 1 Harold Shipman	4
Background and Family	4
Upbringing	5
Schooling	5
Professional Career	6
Murders	8
Investigation and Capture	8
Motivation	11
Trial	11
Aftermath	13
Chapter 2 Donald Harvey	15
Background and Family	15
Upbringing	16
Schooling	17
Professional Career	18
Murders	20
Investigation and Capture	21
Motivation	23
Incarceration	23
Aftermath	24
Chapter 3 Orville Lynn Majors	25
Background and Family	25
Upbringing	26
Schooling	27

Professional Career	27
Murders	27
Investigation and Capture	30
Motivation	31
Trial	33
Aftermath	34

Chapter 4 Jane Toppan — 36

Background and Family	36
Upbringing	37
Schooling	39
Professional Career	40
Murders	41
Investigation and Capture	43
Motivation	44
Trial	46
Aftermath	47

Chapter 5 Stephan Letter — 49

Background and Family	49
Upbringing	50
Schooling	51
Professional Career	52
Murders	53
Investigation and Capture	55
Motivation	56
Trial	58
Aftermath	59

Chapter 6 Arnfinn Nesset — 60

Background and Family	60
Upbringing	61

Schooling	61
Professional Career	62
Murders	63
Investigation and Capture	65
Motivation	66
Trial	67
Aftermath	68
Chapter 7 Roger Andermatt	**69**
Background and Family	69
Upbringing	70
Schooling	71
Professional Career	72
Murders	73
Investigation and Capture	74
Motivation	75
Trial	75
Aftermath	76
Chapter 8 Ludivine Chambet	**78**
Background and Family	78
Upbringing	79
Schooling	81
Professional Career	82
Murders	83
Investigation and Capture	84
Motivation	84
Trial	85
Aftermath	87
Chapter 9 Lucy Letby	**89**
Background and Family	89

Upbringing	90
Schooling	90
Professional Career	91
Murders	93
Investigation and Capture	98
Motivation	103
Trial	104
Aftermath	110
Chapter 10 Charles Cullen	**113**
Background and Family	113
Upbringing	114
Schooling	115
Military Service	118
Nursing School	119
Professional Career	120
Murders	128
Investigation and Capture	132
Motivation	134
Trial	134
Aftermath	135
Conclusion	**137**
References	**139**

Introduction

All serial killers are depraved individuals, but there is something particularly heinous about healthcare workers who take advantage of their caregiver status to commit murder. Patients are often forced to put their complete trust in doctors, nurses, and orderlies, being in a vulnerable position in which they have no way to defend themselves if their caregivers choose to do them harm. The Hippocratic Oath, which requires doctors to prescribe only beneficial care and abstain from causing injury or hurt, is therefore, extremely serious among medical professionals. It is the only safeguard that patients have against mistreatment. If people can't trust those meant to help them, they would never seek out medical care to begin with.

The idea that those sworn to preserve life would be willing to cause death is disturbing, and while cases of it happening are rare, it can still have a profound impact on both the medical community and society at large. Instances of serial killers operating in hospitals, clinics, and other medical facilities have exposed weaknesses in the healthcare system and the legislation surrounding it. Following the capture and conviction of the murderers, laws and regulations are often amended to address the problems that allowed the killers to commit their crimes. This might be of little comfort to the families of the victims, but it at least helps to prevent similar murders from occurring in the future.

A common theme among serial killers in the medical field is that they use the concept of mercy as a shield against those who would deem them cold-blooded murderers. While euthanasia is a controversial topic with plenty of nuance and strong opinions both for and against it, most people can agree that ending someone's life at their own request to ease their suffering is very different from murdering a patient under their care without their consent. No matter how the perpetrator tries to spin it, their crimes are legally and morally inexcusable.

The reasons that lead a person working as a doctor or nurse to become a mass murderer of helpless patients are varied, but many share the quality of stemming from childhood trauma or abuse. Experiencing these things at a young age leaves them feeling helpless, and murdering those in their care can give them a sense of control that they lacked in their lives. In other cases, there were psychopathic or sociopathic elements ingrained in the perpetrators' personalities from a young age. They became fascinated by death and aspired to hold the fate of others in their own hands, making them feel powerful.

Throughout this book, you will discover many similarities between the perpetrators and their motivations that made them become murderers. The psychology of someone who decides it would be permissible to take not just one, but many innocent lives, doesn't come out of nowhere. Something must occur that twists the mind until it views murder as a viable action to take against a victim who cannot even fight back. By uncovering the psychological reasons for these people turning into mass murderers, it's possible to spot early warning signs in others and get them help before they join the ranks of the world's most infamous serial killers.

Chapter 1

Harold Shipman

Harold Shipman was a family physician from England who is widely considered the most prolific serial killer in history. His murders earned him nicknames such as "The Angel of Death," "Dr. Death," and "The Good Doctor". He was believed to have committed at least 250 murders over 23 years, all of which went undetected until his final victim was slain. Shipman's reign of terror resulted in permanent changes to the British medical field, and his memory still hangs like a shadow over the area of Hyde in Greater Manchester, where the majority of his murders occurred.

Background and Family

Harold Frederick Shipman was born on 14 January 1946 in Nottingham, England to Harold Frederick Shipman and Vera Shipman (née Brittan). Despite sharing the same name as his father, Shipman was not a "junior," and was mostly called "Fred" by family and friends. The elder Harold and Vera were a working-class couple, and neither had attended university. Harold drove a lorry for a living, spending long periods of time on the road, leaving the domineering Vera to handle most of their son's upbringing. His disinterest in how his son was raised contributed to the skewed perspective his wife was allowed to cultivate in the boy.

Upbringing

Shipman's parents were Methodists and deeply involved in their local church. Vera viewed herself as morally-superior to others, a trait she instilled in her young son. The idea that they knew better than everyone else what was best became a recurring aspect of Shipman's personality that followed him throughout his entire life. As an adolescent, he rarely had close friends. Part of the reason for this stemmed from his superiority complex, as other children found him to be tiresome and overbearing. However, he was very intelligent and athletically-gifted, dedicating himself to long-distance running and a youth rugby league.

Schooling

In 1957, Shipman entered High Pavement Grammar School in Nottingham after passing the "eleven-plus" standardized tests. He attended this school until 1964, earning the spot as vice-captain of the athletics team during his final year. However, while there, his mother became extremely ill, suffering from lung cancer. Due to the frequent absences of his father, Shipman oversaw her care and was particularly affected by the way morphine treatments were administered to her to ease her suffering. After she succumbed to the disease on 21 June

1963, he shifted his priorities in school, wishing to pursue a career in medicine.

A year after finishing his education at High Pavement, he met a 17-year-old girl named Primrose May Oxtoby at a bus stop near the University of Leeds. They started dating around this time while Shipman was working on achieving his dream of becoming a doctor. Although Shipman failed his first attempt at passing the entrance exam to get into the Leeds School of Medicine at the University of Leeds, he gave it another try and was successful. He began attending medical school in 1966, but his personal life was complicated after Primrose became pregnant. The couple married that same year, only four months before having their first child.

While studying medicine, Shipman got a position as an intern at a local hospital, putting him in direct contact with patients and giving him real-world medical experience. Following four years of intensive training, he graduated from university with his medical degree in 1970. He and Primrose had their second child, and he began searching for opportunities to put his health care knowledge to good use. Some of the issues that would later plague his professional career began to crop up almost immediately, such as his inability to accept when he was wrong. This made it difficult for him to get a permanent job following his graduation.

Professional Career

Shipman's first position as a doctor came when he joined the staff of the Pontefract General Infirmary, located in Pontefract, England. In 1974, he secured a job at the Abraham Ormerod Medical Centre in Todmorden, England, as a general practitioner (GP). His career as a GP got off to an inauspicious start when he was caught forging pethidine prescriptions that he was personally abusing. Pethidine is a synthetic opioid pain medication, often sold under the brand name "Demerol." Following his drug addiction's exposure, he was forced out of his practice and into rehab. Ultimately, he was given a £600 fine for forgery, but didn't lose his ability to practice medicine.

Despite this setback, Shipman was hired at Donneybrook Medical Centre in Hyde, England, in 1977. He again worked as a GP, building up a thriving practice where he had access to a constant stream of patients. Over the next two decades, he embedded himself as a highly-respected member of the medical field and local community. The TV station Granada Television (now ITV Granada) even interviewed him in 1983 for their current affairs program *World in Action*, where he was consulted for his expertise on the community's treatment of the mentally ill. Having become a father of four children and outwardly putting on airs as a devoted family man, Shipman seemed like the perfect representative of Hyde's medical industry.

In 1993, he opened up his own surgery clinic in Hyde, located at 21 Market Street. The shame of his forgery and drug addiction had long since been forgotten. He enjoyed the trust of both patients and colleagues, who viewed him as a hardworking and effective physician. However, much of the junior staff he worked with found him to be unpleasant and arrogant. Once he had earned a positive reputation and a place of esteem amongst his peers, he was able to maintain the facade easily. To him, the opinions of those he saw as beneath him mattered little in the long run, and they didn't have the professional capital to hurt his career.

Murders

The murders committed by Shipman were believed to have started all the way back in 1975, while he was in the midst of his Pethidine addiction. Over his career as both a doctor and a serial killer, he is estimated to have murdered at least 250 people, nearly all of them while under his professional care. This breach of trust is anathema to the medical profession, and it was unthinkable that someone of Shipman's stature as a doctor and elder within the community could commit such heinous crimes. His favored method of murder was inducing a drug overdose in his victims, either by personally administering the medication or overprescribing dangerous substances to at-risk patients.

Investigation and Capture

The first sign of trouble for Shipman came in March 1998, when Dr Linda Reynolds, a member of the Brooke Surgery in Hyde, brought her concerns about the high death rate among Shipman's patients to the South Manchester District's coroner, John Pollard. Shipman had asked her to countersign a suspicious amount of cremation forms for elderly women, much more than the typical death rates for that segment of the population would suggest was normal. When Dr Susan Booth, another of Shipman's colleagues, approached the coroner with similar concerns, Pollard contacted the police. However, a covert investigation failed to turn up evidence against Shipman.

It should have been relatively simple for the authorities to uncover previous instances of wrongdoing and Shipman's criminal record, but they didn't contact the General Medical Council (GMC) during their investigation and never sought to make basic inquiries into his past. Instead, his position as a respected doctor and the word of friends and family helped shield him from suspicion and consequences. Many of his victims' families accepted his official explanations for their loved ones' deaths, and without a more thorough investigation into the matter, it was an uphill battle for the few seeking justice.

Unfortunately for Shipman, Angela Woodruff, the daughter of an 81-year-old victim named Kathleen Grundy, who died on 24 June 1998, refused to believe the doctor's lies. She was a lawyer who had always been in charge of Kathleen's legal affairs, so it shocked her when she discovered her mother had created a new will leaving the majority of the wealthy, elderly widow's estate to Shipman. This didn't sit right with Angela, especially since her mother never expressed her intention to give away her money to her doctor. It all seemed very convenient. Kathleen died immediately after a visit to Shipman, and he had insisted an autopsy wasn't necessary. Given these factors, Angela wasn't willing to take the doctor for his word.

Angela also reviewed the new version of Kathleen's will and felt it was a forgery. She brought the document to the police, and Detective Superintendent Bernard Postles came to the same conclusion following his review of the evidence. Since Kathleen had already been buried, it was exhumed, and an autopsy was performed. It was determined that Kathleen had died from a morphine overdose given to her around three hours prior to her death, which occurred at the same time as Shipman's final visit. The police raided his home and collected a veritable treasure trove of evidence against the doctor. It turned out that Kathleen wasn't his only victim. The floodgates had been opened, and Shipman's world was about to come crashing down around him.

While he had managed to pull the wool over the eyes of patients and fellow doctors alike, Shipman wasn't as smart as he believed when it came to covering his tracks. He altered many of his victims' medical records to support his false claims about their deaths, but failed to realize that each time he logged into the records system to make changes, it was time-stamped. This allowed the authorities to know exactly when he illegally altered patient records, as well as which patients were victims of murder. Shipman also attempted to falsify evidence in a computer medical journal that painted Kathleen as a drug addict, but again, the data proved these were written after she had already died.

On 7 September 1998, Shipman was arrested in connection to Kathleen's death. At this time, the typewriter which was used to forge his victim's will was found, directly linking him to the crime. Patient records seized from the doctor's home showed that Kathleen was far from his only victim, and they began investigating patients who had died shortly after a visit to Shipman, but hadn't been cremated. This led them to charging him for the murder of an additional 14 women, bringing his total to 15 victims. Many were wealthy, sick, and elderly, lacking the ability to keep track of their valuables. Following Shipman's arrest, more than £10,000 in stolen jewelry was recovered from his garage, providing a strong motive for the murders.

Motivation

After seeing how his mother responded to morphine treatments, as well as his own foray into drug abuse, Shipman developed a fascination with controlling physical suffering through incredibly strong pain medications. There was also a significant element of greed to the murders. The jewelry and other valuables he stole were worth a lot of money, and if the will he had forged wasn't outed as a fake, he was set to inherit a sizable fortune from Kathleen's estate. In his mind, they were all old and close to death anyway. His victims had no need for the money, while he was still relatively young and had a large family. Shipman's arrogance meant he believed he was entitled to a larger reward for all the "good" he did, ending his victims' suffering and "caring" for them in their final days.

Trial

Shipman's trial began on 5 October 1999 in Preston Crown Court in Preston, England. He was charged with 15 counts of murder by lethal injection of diamorphine, spanning from 1995 to 1998. There was also a single count of forgery against him for the matter of Kathleen's will. The defense team made an unsuccessful bid to separate Kathleen from the other 14 victims since her case had much stronger evidence and motive attached to it. Because Kathleen was included with the other victims, the crown had an easier time proving Shipman's guilt, as the forged will lent credence to the accusations that the doctor was motivated primarily by greed. The recovered valuables logged as evidence appeared to support this theory.

On 31 January 2000, the jury returned a verdict of guilty for all 15 charges of murder and the single charge of forgery. They had deliberated for six days before reaching a decision. Sir John Thayne Forbes sentenced Shipman to life imprisonment for the 15 counts of murder, while four years of imprisonment for the forgery was to be served concurrently. He recommended that the guilty party be subject to a whole life tariff. David Blunkett, the Home Secretary serving in the Labour administration of Prime Minister Tony Blair, confirmed the whole life tariff in 2002, only a few months before the government lost the power to set minimum terms for prisoner sentences.

Eleven days after his conviction, the GMC removed Shipman's name from the medical register. He remains the only doctor in British history convicted for murdering their own patients. The only other doctor charged was John Bodkin Adams, who was accused of killing a single patient in 1957, but was subsequently acquitted of the crime. While Adams was rumored to have killed dozens of patients, his acquittal prevented the necessity of reform until Shipman was convicted. Her Majesty's Prison Service remanded Shipman to HM Prison Wakefield, where he was set to live out the rest of his natural life.

Aftermath

In 2001, a senior West Yorkshire Police detective named Chris Gregg was chosen to serve as the head of an investigation into 22 local deaths of Shipman's patients. The investigation resulted in the determination that the doctor had committed 218 murders between 1975 and 1998, covering the period when he worked in both Todmorden and Hyde. There were additional suspicious deaths for which Shipman was believed to be responsible, but this could not be proved beyond reasonable doubt. In early 2005, judge Dame Janet Smith submitted a report ascribing between three to seven suspicious deaths to Shipman during the early stages of his career in Pontefract, including that of a 4-year-old girl.

Early in the morning on 13 January 2004, Shipman's body was found hanging with a bedsheet around his neck that had been secured to the bars of his cell's window. At the time of his suicide, he was 57 years old. Because he refused to confess to his crimes, the families of his victims felt like they were cheated out of the satisfaction of hearing the truth from his own mouth. Some of the valuables recovered from Shipman's home during the murder investigation were returned to the owners' families when they could be definitively identified, while Primrose was given 66 pieces. A further 33 pieces were confirmed to not belong to her, but their provenance was never ascertained. They were later auctioned off, with the proceeds going to benefit the Tameside Victim Support.

As a result of the Shipman case, a report known as the *Shipman Inquiry* made recommendations to reform standard medical practices across the United Kingdom. This led to a shift from single-doctor to multiple-doctor general practices, preventing a situation where lack of oversight and unfettered, exclusive access to patients could lead to similar instances of abuse. Many doctors have also altered their prescribing habits, dispensing pain medications in a much more conservative manner than before. There was also a change in how death certificates are processed. Overall, this has been dubbed "The Shipman Effect," since these reforms were a direct response to the revelation of his many crimes throughout his professional career.

Chapter 2

Donald Harvey

Known by the self-applied sobriquet "Angel of Death," Donald Harvey was a hospital orderly and nurse's aide responsible for murdering between 37 to 57 victims. However, some estimates place that number as high as 87. His killing spree was carried out from 1970 to 1987 across the American Midwest. Harvey spent much of his time as a serial killer working in hospitals in the cities of London, Kentucky, and Cincinnati, Ohio. Even though he attempted to justify his murders as acts of mercy, it was later determined that he was motivated by much baser instincts for slaughtering dozens of people.

Background and Family

Donald Harvey was born on 15 April 1952 in Hamilton, Ohio, to Ray and Goldie Harvey. At the time of his birth, Ray was 32 years old, while his mother was only 17—a concerning age gap even back during the middle of the 20th century. Harvey's father was a construction worker, while his mother ostensibly stayed at home to raise him. However, she was very ill most of the time, and without Ray around to help her with their newborn baby, she struggled to provide proper care. They weren't able to afford childcare, and they didn't have family or friends nearby who could offer any assistance.

Upbringing

Harvey's family lived well beneath the poverty line throughout his entire childhood. Not long after he was born, they moved from Hamilton to Booneville, Kentucky, a small town in the Appalachian mountains named for the famous American frontiersman Daniel Boone. Goldie's family lived in the area, where they ran a struggling tobacco farm. Ray continued to work in construction, but the lack of opportunities around Booneville forced him to spend three weeks each month away on job sites. This left Harvey, and later his two younger siblings, in the care of extended family during his father's frequent absences.

The majority of Harvey's upbringing was provided by Goldie's parents. He and his siblings typically stayed with their grandparents while Ray was away, and Goldie's brother was often present in the household during these periods. According to Harvey, both his uncle and a neighbor of his grandparents began sexually abusing him when he was 5 years old. This continued until late in his teenage years, and the only person he ever spoke to about it was his sister after the abuse had ended. Because this revelation only came to light following Harvey's arrest, it was never corroborated by other sources, including the sister he had allegedly previously informed about the situation.

As a child, Harvey didn't have many friends and was not liked by his peers. His self-professed preference for performing housework and close relationship to his mother resulted in people deeming him a "mama's boy" and a "sissy." This only served to further his social isolation. In spite of the issues he had with interpersonal relationships, he was actually a competent student, achieving good grades. Many of the problems Harvey experienced later in life stemmed from his difficult childhood, as well as the fact that he realized early on that he was a homosexual. Rural Kentucky in the 1960s and 1970s was not a bastion of progressive thought, so the traits and behavior he exhibited related to his homosexuality caused a significant amount of bullying and ostracization from his community.

Schooling

The majority of Harvey's education occurred in Booneville, both at the local secondary schools and his family's church. While he was relatively intelligent and successful in school, the dire financial circumstances his family experienced forced him to drop out in the middle of ninth grade. His absent father could not make ends meet alone, so he went to work at a nearby factory to help support himself, his siblings, and his chronically-ill mother. Harvey's lack of a high school diploma severely limited his career prospects, so he took a correspondence course to earn his GED, which he achieved in 1968.

Although he had harbored dreams of becoming a doctor, his lack of a formal college education made it impossible. His poverty also hindered his prospects—

even if he could have gotten a full scholarship to attend an accredited university, he couldn't afford to stop working a full-time job. There was also more trouble at home as he got older. When his parents discovered that he was a homosexual, their relationship deteriorated to the point that Harvey decided to leave home at the age of 17. He moved to London, Kentucky to stay with his paternal grandfather.

Professional Career

In 1970, while living with his grandfather, Harvey met a hospital orderly who helped him get a job as a ward clerk at Marymount Hospital. This seemed like a good compromise to his ambitions to become a doctor. It allowed him to work in the medical field without requiring a significant investment of time and money to earn both an undergraduate and medical degree. Moving out of his grandfather's house, he started renting an apartment near the hospital and was able to spend his wages on himself for the first time. He ostensibly enjoyed his new career, but trouble followed Harvey everywhere he went.

Early in 1971, after working at the hospital for barely more than a year, he was arrested for setting a neighboring apartment on fire and burglarizing another neighbor. Being about a month shy of turning 19, Harvey lost his job and was facing serious criminal charges. After a conversation with his father, he decided to join the military. He enlisted in the United States Air Force, receiving an assignment as a clerk and typist. While his enlistment occurred during the height of the Vietnam War, Harvey had lucked out in drawing a relatively safe posting. Unfortunately, the disciplined lifestyle of the military clashed with his personality, and he struggled to adapt.

Harvey only spent nine months in the U.S. Air Force before being discharged. During his tenure, he attempted suicide twice by overdosing on drugs and experienced a nervous breakdown. Following his return home, he overdosed again as part of a third attempted suicide, this time because of the shame brought upon his family due to his multiple suicide attempts while serving in the military. He entered an inpatient psychiatric facility for 4 months and attended outpatient treatment appointments for 18 months after he was released.

Once he had completed his psychiatric treatment, Harvey resumed working at various hospitals as an orderly. In 1975, he got a job at the Cincinnati V.A. Medical Hospital, a veteran's hospital in Cincinnati, Ohio. He eventually switched from being a ward clerk to an autopsy assistant, holding the position for 8 years. About halfway through his time as an autopsy assistant in 1978, he met a man named Carl Hoeweler. They began to date, and Harvey moved into Carl's home. Carl also rented out rooms of his house to tenants as individual apartments, many with whom Harvey did not get along.

Harvey and Carl later split up in 1985, and later that year, Harvey lost his job when slides of human tissue and syringes from the morgue, books containing disturbing occultist subject matter, and an illegal firearm were found in his possession. However, in 1986, he managed to secure a new position as a nurse's aide at Cincinnati Drake Memorial Hospital, a different medical facility in the city.

His new employers failed to perform a background check that would have alerted them to his previous crimes and firings. Drake primarily served elderly and terminally-ill patients. His behavior caused his coworkers to become concerned, and this eventually led to his downfall.

Murders

Throughout his entire healthcare career, he committed a series of murders that would remain secret for 17 years. Part of this was due to the fact that he often changed the means he used to kill his victims, and there was no discernable motive for many of his crimes. According to Harvey, he first began murdering while working at Marymount Hospital. Over a 10-month period, he claimed to have killed 13 victims, but these remained unnoticed until his arrest years later. His first victim was an 88-year-old man named Logan Evans, who was smothered with a plastic bag and pillow. This was supposedly a snap-decision done to ease Logan's suffering.

James Tyree, Harvey's second victim, was a 69-year-old man who was accidentally given the wrong catheter, resulting in James vomiting blood and dying. It was the first of only 4 accidental deaths committed by Harvey out of his 47 confirmed victims. James died while a 12-year-old boy named Danny George was in the room, and Harvey showed a callous flippancy when later recounting the fact to investigators. Later victims were murdered by arsenic, cyanide, and other poisons; intentional drug overdoses using morphine and insulin; suffocation; turning off ventilators; purposely injecting patients with fluids tainted by HIV and/or hepatitis B; and inserting a coat hanger into a patient's catheter, puncturing the abdomen and causing peritonitis.

Not all of Harvey's victims were patients. It was later revealed that from early on in his relationship with Carl, he began secretly administering arsenic to his boyfriend. Supposedly, he wasn't trying to kill Carl, only wanting him to become sick enough that he would remain at home. Several of those Harvey murdered were connected to Carl, including tenants Helen Metzger and Edgar Wilson, an employee who Harvey dosed with hepatitis, but survived her hospitalization, and Carl's own parents. Carl's father, Henry Hoeweler, died from the poisoning, but his mother survived. Another man, Howard Vetter, was killed by accident when he drank alcohol Harvey had poisoned with the intention of murdering an unknown target.

Harvey's final victim was a man named John Powell, who had spent several months on life support after getting into a serious motorcycle accident. John suddenly died without an obvious cause, so an autopsy was performed. Despite being in a coma, it was discovered that he had a significant amount of cyanide in his system. In light of his condition, it was clear that he could not have self-administered the poison. Adding John's death to numerous other suspicious deaths in the hospital, an investigation was launched to ascertain the culprit.

Investigation and Capture

As the death toll at Drake quickly rose, the nurses and his fellow aides voiced their opinion to the administration that he was possibly responsible. The hospital ignored their suspicions, and nothing was done at the time. Following John Powell's suspicious death, they performed an internal investigation and uncovered Harvey's sordid past which was overlooked due to the lack of a proper vetting process for orderlies. He confessed to killing John, but insisted that he'd used the cyanide to euthanize his victim and spare him from further suffering.

While putting together a story about the murder for WCPO-TV, a local news station, reporter and news anchor, Pat Minarcin thought it unlikely that a healthcare professional with nearly two decades of experience in the field would suddenly commit a single murder. He decided to probe deeper into Harvey's past and asked live on the air for any information concerning other possible deaths connected to Harvey. The nurses and aides who had previously reported Harvey to the hospital contacted Minarcin and explained the situation to him. The station did their own investigation and eventually aired a story about the suspicious deaths at Drake as a follow-up to the report about John Powell's murder.

Once their hand was forced by the media, the hospital administration contacted the authorities to begin a formal criminal investigation. Minarcin's story accused Harvey of committing 24 murders within 4 years and theorized that he was able to get away with it for so long because he was killing victims who were old or terminally-ill and therefore, expected to die. Harvey was arrested on

6 April 1987, shortly after Minarcin's follow-up story, and eventually confessed to murdering around 60 victims. Many of his victims could not be identified or definitively linked to Harvey, and he was eventually charged with 37 murders.

Motivation

Initially, Harvey claimed that his primary motivation was to end the suffering of his victims. However, after John Powell's murder brought to light many more victims, including a handful who weren't his patients, this lie fell apart. He later admitted that most of the people he killed were due to anger or jealousy. This included patients who got on his bad side, acquaintances he frequently argued with, and anyone his ex-boyfriend Carl lavished attention upon. Following a court-ordered psychiatric evaluation, the psychiatrist stated their belief that many of his murders were committed as a way to relieve tension and ease his own mental suffering. He didn't want to have to feel negative emotions, so he opted to remove those he perceived as the cause of those emotions.

Incarceration

Harvey's case never went to trial. He instead agreed to a plea bargain with both the Cincinnati District Attorney and the Laurel County Circuit Court in Kentucky, pleading guilty to 37 murders, including 24 counts of first-degree murder. In accordance with the deal, Harvey admitted to every murder he committed, and the death penalty would be taken off the table. However, the D.A. reserved the right to return the death penalty to the table if any more murders came to light. He was sentenced to three life sentences for the murders in Ohio and life plus 20 years for the murders in Kentucky, with both sentences to run concurrently.

Aftermath

On 26 October 1987, Harvey entered the Ohio prison system, serving out his sentence at the Toledo Correctional Institution. His severely-beaten body was found in his cell on 28 March 2017, almost 40 years exactly from when he committed his final murder. He died two days later from the injuries sustained during the attack. Fellow inmate James Elliot was charged on 3 May 2019 for aggravated murder, as well as additional charges in relation to Harvey's death, and he pleaded guilty in September 2019. In the end, Harvey suffered the same fate that he doled out to dozens of innocent victims during his career as a caregiver.

Chapter 3

Orville Lynn Majors

Orville Lynn Majors was a nurse who is believed to have killed over 100 victims during his short healthcare career in Indiana. He was a man of two faces—the sweet, nurturing medical professional and a vicious, bloodthirsty serial killer. Unlike many other serial killers, Majors did not come from a particularly poor or abusive family, and he never claimed to have suffered any significant traumas as a child. His reasons for committing murder are, therefore, harder to trace back to a specific cause, making his case very interesting from a psychological standpoint.

Background and Family

Orville Lynn Majors was born on 24 April 1961 in Linton, Indiana, to Orville Gene and Anna Bell Majors (née Reeves). The elder Orville was a coal miner, and Anna owned multiple different types of businesses throughout her life, including a pet shop, flower shop, and antique store. While Anna's family was from Muhlenberg County, Kentucky, Orville's came from Vermillion County, Indiana. Majors' parents were both Baptists, with Anna being far more integrated into the church than her husband. Orville's mother—Majors' paternal grandmother—lived nearby, but suffered from chronic ailments that kept her bedridden most of the time.

Upbringing

Majors had a relatively normal childhood for the American midwest in the second half of the 20th century. Anna insisted that her two children be brought up within the faith, and forced Majors and his sister Debbie to attend services with her. Orville was less enthusiastic about his family's churchgoing activities and rarely went with them. As a result, the majority of the children's religious ideals were influenced by their mother's stricter beliefs. Part of the religious doctrine to which Anna subscribed included caring for the sick and infirm, a fact that was responsible for Majors' decision to pursue a career as a healthcare worker.

As a teenager, his paternal grandmother became too ill to care for herself, leading Majors to take over as her informal nurse. This experience was pivotal in his decision to join the medical industry as a professional nurse. However, it also provided the first instance of contradictory viewpoints when it came to his feelings on the elderly. He was raised to see caring for elderly and ailing individuals as a virtue, and strived to live up to that ideal, yet he simultaneously was revolted by the way they couldn't take care of themselves, as well as the habits, behaviors, and symptoms presented by such people. His inability to reconcile this internal conflict later caused many innocent victims to lose their lives.

Schooling

Majors attended secondary school in Linton, where he was a decent student and relatively well-liked by his peers. According to a high school classmate named Amy McCombs, "He was like a big teddy bear. He was a very likable guy who was always laughing and making people feel better." It made sense to friends and family that Majors would dedicate his life to caring for the needs of others. Nobody was surprised when he packed up and moved to Nashville, Tennessee, to take classes at the Nashville Memorial School of Practical Nursing. After completing their program, he graduated with his nursing degree in 1989.

Professional Career

Following his graduation, Majors returned to Indiana and got a position as a licensed practical nurse at Vermillion County Hospital (VCH), located north of Terre Haute in the small town of Clinton. VCH wasn't a large facility, only having 56 beds and a 4-bed intensive care unit. Outside of his duties at the hospital, he also worked for a home healthcare agency as a visiting nurse, and helped out with his mother's pet shop. For a brief period, Majors secured a job in Tennessee that paid much more than VCH, but he chafed working in a larger place with tougher demands and more oversight. In 1993, he returned to Clinton and was rehired at VCH, where he stayed for the remainder of his career.

Murders

The first murder committed by Majors occurred after he went back to VCH. Unlike in Tennessee, he had the complete trust of his supervisors, who allowed him to treat patients without keeping a close eye on his activities. The number of patients at the hospital who died each year averaged around 26, yet it skyrocketed to over 100 in 1993 and 1994. At one point, one out of every three patients admitted to the hospital ended up dying. There was no clear reason for this sudden and drastic change, causing administrators to scramble in an attempt to stem the tide of death sweeping through their halls.

Despite the fact that this alarming statistic coincided with Majors' 22-month tenure after returning from Tennessee, nobody connected him to the crimes for a while. When dealing with patients, he displayed a caring and sensitive bedside manner that put people at ease. To all outward appearances, he was the perfect nurse, and the families of patients felt very comfortable giving him unsupervised access to their loved ones. He took advantage of this free rein to murder his victims with lethal doses of epinephrine and potassium chloride.

Majors was able to ward off suspicion in the beginning because most of his victims were elderly and already sick. Taken as isolated incidents, the deaths themselves weren't a cause for immediate concern. However, there were indications that something darker lurked beneath the surface of those who died at VCH. Majors was treating a 56 year old patient named Freddie Dale Wilson, and injected a substance unknown to his daughter, who was also present in the room. Within moments, Freddie was dead, and while the hospital chalked it up to an unfortunate coincidence, the victim's family wasn't convinced this was true.

Some of Majors' co-workers began to notice how often he was around when patients died. He joked about knowing when the next death would happen, which disturbed the other nurses and aides. Andy Harris, who lived with Majors around the time of the murders, reportedly heard him say things like, "Old people should be gassed." It seemed like there were two completely different sides to him—one that offered tender treatment to his patients, and the other that showed a callous disdain for their well-being behind their backs.

In 1995, Dawn Stirek, a nursing supervisor at VCH, heard enough whispers about Majors' behavior to make her suspicious. After checking the duty roster and staff time cards, she discovered, to her horror, that Majors was on duty during 130 of the 147 deaths that occurred between his rehiring in 1993 and 1995. It was no longer possible to ignore the situation, and the hospital administration suspended him after contacting the Indiana State Police. His suspension was initially temporary, pending the results of an investigation.

An internal investigation was conducted, and it was found that Majors had exceeded his authority by working in the ICU and administering emergency drugs without the presence of a doctor. This was the exact issue that had drawn Majors back to VCH from Tennessee, because his former employers refused to give him the same type of leeway that VCH did. While it's unclear whether the administration was aware that Majors was allowed to operate with so little oversight, they laid all the blame at his feet to avoid questions of their own culpability. VCH fired him, and the police began probing into the nature of the deaths.

Investigation and Capture

Once the Indiana State Police investigated Majors' activities, they found that a disturbing pattern emerged: when he was off-duty, there was about 1 death every 23 days, but anytime he was on duty, it became 1 death every 23 hours. A patient who entered VCH while Majors was working was 42 times more likely to never leave again. Even though these facts made it obvious that he was responsible for the catastrophic death rate, he adamantly denied any wrongdoing. Thanks to his mother's multiple successful businesses, he was able to hire an expensive lawyer who initiated a blitz campaign to get out ahead of the allegations.

While the police investigation was still in its infancy, Majors toured the area, making talk show appearances where he loudly insisted to viewers that he was innocent and being railroaded by the authorities. The police struggled to get their case in order against him, even though they were absolutely convinced he was a murderer, they lacked the evidence to prove how he killed his victims. They might have never learned the truth if not for Majors' high-profile media visibility. After seeing him on television, the families of his victims contacted the police to inform them about the suspicious behavior he exhibited while treating their loved ones shortly before victims died.

Like with Freddie Wilson, other family members recalled seeing Majors administer injections of some kind. The patients coded shortly after these injections, with some dying before Majors had even departed from the room. This commonality led investigators to take a closer look at potential medications that would cause near-instantaneous death. At the same time, a medical investigation team discovered that many patients had widening heart patterns on their EKGs around the time of death. Three possible explanations were offered: a sudden heart attack, large clot in the lungs, or potassium overdose.

Following the exhumation and autopsy of 15 patients who exhibited suspicious EKG activity, it was determined that none of them suffered from a heart attack or lung clots. This left only a potassium overdose as their cause of death, which meant they were murdered. Andy Harris reported to police that he remembered Majors keeping vials of epinephrine and potassium chloride in their home when they lived together. The authorities obtained a warrant and searched Majors' current residence, where they located vials of the same drugs that originated from VCH. Combined with the witnesses who personally saw Majors administer injections to the victims right before they died, the police finally had the evidence they needed to charge the culprit.

Motivation

Most of Majors' victims were targeted because he allegedly found them to be whiny and demanding, or their healthcare needs caused his workload to be unnecessarily increased. He secretly despised the patients he treated, and yet still had the urge to continue serving as a hospital nurse. Some psychiatrists who did not treat Majors but analyzed his history and behavior, speculated that the religious ideals instilled within him by his mother made him feel compelled to continue providing care to those he hated.

Because the murders only began after Majors was rehired at VCH in 1993, there were questions about what triggered the serial killings. It was assumed that he had held the same negative perspective on elderly patients since as far back as his time caring for his grandmother, but it wasn't until after his temporary relocation to the new job in Tennessee that he realized he could actually get away with carrying out what had previously remained contained to the realm of fantasy: revenge slayings.

The freedom afforded to him when dealing with patients at VCH meant that he was often left alone when treating patients, including being in charge of the types of medication they were given. With nobody looking over his shoulder, he could administer anything he wanted to a patient that annoyed him, and because he always acted caring in front of others, nobody would suspect him of murder. It's very possible that he became emboldened by how easily he killed such a massive number of victims right under everyone's noses for nearly two years. When the accusations against him led to his suspension, instead of remaining quiet, he believed he could outsmart the world by going on television to maintain his innocence. This ironically had the complete opposite effect.

Trial

It took two years for the police investigation into Majors to conclude, resulting in his arrest in December 1997. While the authorities suspected he was responsible for anywhere between 100 and 130 deaths, the prosecution didn't want to overwhelm the jury, and chose to focus on the deaths with the strongest evidence. He was charged with seven murders, including Mary Ann Alderson, age 69; Dorothea Hixon, age 80; Cecil Smith, age 74; Luella Hopkins, age 89; Margaret Hornick, age 79; Derek Maxwell, Sr., age 64; and Freddie Wilson. There were 79 witnesses who testified against Majors, such as his former roommate, who repeated the claim that the accused killer hated elderly people and thought they should be "gassed."

Majors' defense team attempted to paint the deaths as being due to natural causes, calling in experts to testify that the victims had preexisting conditions that made it likely they would have died regardless of external intervention. There was also a suggestion that Majors was unjustly targeted by the police, with many other doctors and nurses having access to the same patients as their client. They claimed that VCH had called on Majors to exceed his authority due to not keeping enough doctors on staff legally permitted to provide necessary care to patients, and that because the hospital didn't want to spend additional money, the options were to either overstep his authority to treat the patients, or neglect their care and allow them to die.

On 17 October 1997, the jury returned a guilty verdict on six of the seven counts of murder. The last charge resulted in a deadlock, since the victim did not die as quickly as the others. Majors was sentenced to serve six consecutive 60-year terms in prison, with 60 years being the maximum penalty allowed by Indiana law at the time of the verdict. In essence, this was considered a life sentence, and it was reasonably assumed that Majors would die before serving it completely. Ernest Yelton, the judge who presided over the trial, was frustrated by the lack of a true life sentence, stating, "The maximum sentence is the minimum sentence in this case." He called the murders diabolical acts," and "a parallel of evil at its most wicked."

Aftermath

In an effort to distance themselves from the stain on their reputation brought on by Majors' serial murders, VCH renamed themselves to West Central Community Hospital. They were hit with 80 wrongful death lawsuits filed by the families of Majors' victims, and settled with the complainants in most cases. The hospital was also fined $80,000 for code violations and negligence. VCH was forced to shut down for a brief period after losing its accreditation as a result of the fines and lawsuits. In 2009, the hospital was sold to the Terre Haute-based Union Hospital, and was renamed again to Union Hospital Clinton.

Majors attempted to appeal his conviction with the Indiana Supreme Court, but they upheld the guilty verdict in 2002. He served his sentence in the Indiana State

Prison, a major criminal penitentiary in Michigan City. On 24 September 2017, Majors got into a heated argument with a corrections officer named R. Houston. In the middle of the conflict, the prisoner suffered a heart attack, and was pronounced dead soon after. He was 56 years old when he died, having spent the previous 20 years in prison. Ultimately, the 60-year sentences proved to be a life sentence for Majors.

Chapter 4

Jane Toppan

Jane Toppan was a professional nurse and serial killer whose spree of murders occurred in Massachusetts from 1895 to 1901. Throughout her career, she claimed to have killed more than 30 people, but she was ultimately charged with 12 counts of murder. She tried to present her crimes as being motivated by a compulsion to become an "angel of mercy," but her actions proved otherwise. There were much more personal reasons for her serial killings, and her inability to recognize that fact contributed to a spate of murders in a very brief stretch of time. She was an otherwise intelligent woman, and if she was as sane as she believed, it would've been obvious that her crimes would eventually catch up to her.

Background and Family

Jane Toppan was born as Honora Kelley on 31 March 1854 in Boston, Massachusetts, to Peter and Bridget Kelley. Both of her parents were Irish immigrants, and they had a large number of children in a very short span of time. Toppan was the youngest of their brood, and Bridget died from tuberculosis only a few years after she was born. Her father struggled to hold down a steady job, and he left his younger children in the care of the older ones who remained at home. However, most of them left the moment an opportunity presented itself, and it wasn't long before he no longer possessed the means to care for those who remained behind.

Not much is known about Toppan's siblings, with only the barest of information concerning the fates of her elder sisters, Nellie and Delia. The Kelley family was very poor, as was typical for a sizable portion of mid-19th century immigrants living in the United States. Boston was famous for its Irish population, but without the economic and infrastructural support necessary to comfortably maintain the influx of newcomers to the city, many were unable to find proper jobs or housing, being forced to live in overcrowded apartments or on the streets.

Upbringing

Toppan's mother provided the majority of house and child care for the Kelley family, so when she died, Peter was unable to keep his children together. In 1860, he turned over his youngest two daughters—6-year-old Toppan and 8-year-old Delia—to the Boston Female Asylum. This was an orphanage meant for indigent children, and records concerning the girls' arrival noted that they were "rescued from a very miserable home." Peter was an alcoholic who was known to be both abusive and mentally ill. Later in life, while he was working as a tailor, he ended up sewing both of his own eyelids shut.

Nellie inherited her father's mental illnesses, resulting in her being committed to an insane asylum, where she later died. Delia became a prostitute after leaving the orphanage, and she contracted various diseases that led to her dying relatively young amidst destitution. Within two years of Peter sending his daughters to the orphanage, Toppan was given to the family of Ann C. Toppan to work as an indentured servant. Ann's family lived in the nearby city of Lowell, and were much wealthier than the Kelley family. Despite her position as a servant, Toppan enjoyed far more favorable living conditions than she ever did with the Kelleys or at the orphanage.

Hoping to distance herself from her origins, especially her father, whose public reputation as an "eccentric alcoholic" earned him the nickname "Kelley the Crack," Toppan changed her first name to "Jane" and adopted her benefactors' surname. While presenting herself as "Jane Toppan," she would allow others to infer that she was Ann's daughter, as the Toppan family actually had a daughter named Elizabeth. However, Toppan tried not to outright lie to anyone, relying on vague comments and answers to lead those she met to draw the conclusion themselves. This way, if the truth was discovered, she could claim it was a simple misunderstanding. Since she was on good terms with Elizabeth, there never seemed to be any hard feelings about possible mix-ups, and nobody discovered that Toppan's intentions were anything less than pure.

The harsh conditions and uncertain circumstances she was subjected to in her youth forged a talent for lying and surreptitiousness in the young girl. She understood that her survival was entirely dependent on her ability to get others to like her and want to offer her assistance. She developed a good-natured false front that made her appear very sweet, caring, and likable. This prevented her from following her elder sisters into the squalor and the unfortunate directions their lives eventually took. Toppan wasn't afraid to take advantage of others, although she did her best to disguise her behavior to avoid suspicion. Any wrongdoing always occurred in such a way that she could claim innocence, with people usually believing her lies.

Schooling

The Toppan family was generous to their indentured servant, helping her receive a formal education that would have otherwise been denied to her. She was very intelligent and hard-working, which made her a far more dangerous individual than most realized. In 1885, she was accepted into the training program at Cambridge Hospital, where she studied to become a nurse. Her patients and co-workers fell for the facade she put on as a bright, cheerful, and friendly caregiver, to the point that she was dubbed "Jolly Jane" by those around her.

There were select patients with whom she would become very close, most being the elderly and infirm. These patients were quietly subjected to horrific experimentation by Toppan, usually because she wished to see how they responded to certain treatment options. Her favorite experiments involved using morphine and atropine, with the goal being to study how the drugs affected the patients' nervous systems. Because she wasn't keeping official records of her experiments, their purpose was not meant to benefit the medical community at large—instead, it was for personal knowledge and a thirst to inflict harm upon other human beings.

Toppan was given significant leeway with patients, often providing treatment on her own, which allowed her to alter their dosage amounts, forge phony medical charts, and administer drugs in such a manner that they would be in and out of consciousness. She would even climb into bed with them and molest them for her own sexual gratification. Throughout her entire residency at Cambridge, her sick experiments and disturbing behavior was never discovered. Outside of her genial personality, she was able to evade suspicion because most of her victims were too old and sick to truly understand what was happening to them.

Professional Career

In 1889, following the completion of her residency at Cambridge, Toppan was recommended to Massachusetts General Hospital. This was a prestigious teaching hospital that was part of Harvard University, and it spoke to the amount of respect she had garnered during her training and residency. However, after only working there for a year, she was fired. Her experimentation and bizarre behavior was not overlooked at Massachusetts General the way it had been at Cambridge.

Being well-liked at Cambridge, Toppan was able to return there as a professional nurse. They hired her on the strength of her previous performance with them, unable to understand why Massachusetts General fired her. Not everyone at the hospital was blinded by her public persona in the same way as the administration. There were some co-workers who were more wary of her, especially due to the rumors they heard through the nursing grapevine. Because she had previously enjoyed such a free hand at Cambridge, she ramped up her activities, but overplayed her hand. While the true nature of her crimes weren't discovered, she was caught overprescribing opiates and dismissed from her position.

Despite losing her job, Toppan was not barred from practicing as a caregiver. This let her move into a career as a private nurse, where her intelligence and personality helped her flourish. While there were some complaints leveled against her concerning instances of petty theft, the lack of hard evidence and her competence while on the job smoothed over any potential problems that cropped up. Working in private residences with little oversight made it much easier for her to carry out her experiments unhindered. This made it all too easy for Toppan to shift her crimes from abuse to outright murder.

Murders

The first known victims of Toppan's killing spree were her landlord, the 83-year-old Israel Dunham, and his 87-year-old wife ,Lovely. She secretly administered poison to the couple while serving as their nurse, and Israel was the first to die. He succumbed to the poisoning on 26 May 1895. Lovely was murdered a little over two years later, on 19 September 1897. Due to their age and need for a private nurse, nobody thought it was strange that the couple died. This allowed Toppan to move on to more victims without anyone catching on at the time.

Her next victim was Elizabeth Brigham, the daughter of Ann Toppan and her foster sister. She murdered the 70-year-old Elizabeth on 29 August 1899 by poisoning her with a dosage of strychnine. As a white, odorless, and bitter-tasting powder substance, Toppan administered the poison by placing it in her victim's coffee. Although Elizabeth wasn't known to be ill at the time, the symptoms of strychnine poisoning aren't specific enough to be recognized by observation, and there was no reason to run a toxicology examination on the victim upon her death.

Toppan soon murdered two more people connected to her foster sister: Florence Calkins, who was Elizabeth's 45-year-old former housekeeper, and Edna Bannister, Elizabeth's 77-year-old sister-in-law. Florence was killed on 15 January 1900, while Edna succumbed to Toppan's machinations on 19 June 1901. On 28 December 1899, in between the deaths of Elizabeth and Florence, Toppan murdered a 70-year-old patient named Mary McNear. After killing Florence, but before Edna died, she also murdered two other patients: 70-year-old William Ingraham on 27 January 1900, and 48-year-old Sarah "Myra" Connors on 11 February 1900. Myra happened to consider Toppan a friend, so her family didn't blame the nurse for their loved one's death.

The last four victims in Toppan's career as a serial killer all came from the Davis family. On 4 July 1901, she used an Independence Day celebration as a cover to murder Mattie Davis, the 62-year-old wife of a wealthy man from Cataumet, Massachusetts. Mattie's widow, Alden Davis, hired Toppan to become his live-in nurse, as Mattie had previously taken care of him, and he required a new caregiver now that she was dead. He believed he could trust her, because his sister was Edna Bannister, who was married to the brother of Toppan's foster sister's husband.

Only a few weeks after moving into the Davis household, Toppan murdered Alden and Mattie's daughter, Genevieve "Annie" Gordon, on 30 July 1901. Alden himself was killed a little over a week later on 8 August 1901, at the age of 64. Toppan's final victim was Mary "Minnie" Gibbs, Alden and Mattie's other daughter, who was 40 years old when she was killed on 13 August 1901, a mere five days after her father. Having four members of the family wiped out in such a short timespan made relatives suspect foul play, and they insisted that a toxicology examination be performed on Minnie. It found that the victim had been poisoned, and the most obvious suspect was Toppan.

Investigation and Capture

Police began quietly watching Toppan to observe her actions and behavior in the time following the murders of the Davis family. They watched her until 29 October 1901, when they finally felt they'd gotten enough evidence to move in and arrest her. At first, Toppan tried to proclaim her innocence, but with so many people dying to whom she was personally connected, many who weren't already sick like most of her patients that were killed, made it impossible to continue denying the truth.

In 1902, she finally confessed to the crimes, even claiming that she'd murdered 31 victims while working at the hospitals and as a private nurse. The veracity of the murders committed at Cambridge and Massachusetts General could not be confirmed, since too many other healthcare professionals had access to the same patients and drugs used by Toppan, so the authorities focused their attention on her victims while serving as a private nurse. In most of these instances, she was the only one with the required background knowledge and easy access to the poisons used as murder weapons.

Motivation

According to Toppan, her experiments on patients at Cambridge and Massachusetts General were done for the purpose of better understanding the way that certain drugs interacted with the human body, and she was searching for a painless method of euthanizing victims whose suffering could not be alleviated by then-current medical technology. This claim falls apart when looking at who her victims were and how she chose to kill them, since most of her proven murders utilized poisons that caused significant trauma to the body and mind.

Delving deeper into her motives show that most of her murders came from anger and jealousy. Toppan reportedly felt like she was inferior to many of her victims due to her Irish heritage, and this provided at least a partial motivation for her murders. In particular, she both hated and wished to be her foster sister, Elizabeth. Many of her victims were associated with Elizabeth in some way, and even Toppan's choice of adopting the persona of "Jane Toppan" was an expression of her desires.

As a private nurse, her patients came from wealthy backgrounds, having the kind of stable, financially secure lives that Toppan could never hope to achieve. She was from a poor immigrant family, and after being sent to the orphanage, every family she lived with came with the caveat that she was essentially a servant. The Toppans never formally adopted her, and she felt that in spite of their generosity, she was never truly treated as an equal. Elizabeth had everything Toppan could only dream of having, including supportive parents with plenty of money and a large group of people who loved her.

There was also an element of greed in Toppan's crimes. Almost immediately after entering her private nursing career, she started to steal from her patients. At the start, it was never anything of enough value to warrant a police report, and much of her greed manifested in non-material gains. In one case, Toppan used non-fatal poisoning as a means to get a housekeeper out of the way and steal her job. She also murdered Mattie Davis to worm her way into Alden's household. Allegedly, Toppan would even poison herself to appear frail and vulnerable, encouraging the men who courted her to go to extra lengths to care for her and offer their assistance.

The most disturbing aspect of Toppan's motives was her admission that she indulged her sexual fetishes at the expense of her victims. She became aroused by her patients being close to death, which was why she would often use drugs to take them to the brink before reviving them. Toppan reportedly enjoyed giving her victims a cocktail of different drugs so she could lay beside them as they died, holding them close to her while the life faded from their eyes. During this time, she would molest them, claiming that she believed she could see the "inner workings of their souls" while in such a heightened emotional state.

Considering the fact that the majority of Toppan's victims were female, and she was never married or had a serious long-term relationship with a man, it's very possible that she harbored homosexual desires that could not be freely expressed in 19th century and early-20th century America. While her family was not particularly religious, the staunch opposition to homosexuality ingrained in the Irish Catholic cultural psyche of Irish-American immigrant culture very well could have played a part in Toppan's internal conflict. In addition to all the other reasons she was jealous of Elizabeth, her foster sister was happily married, something which Toppan might have wanted, but was the antithesis of her inner desires.

Trial

Toppan's trial took place at the Barnstable County Courthouse in 1902. It concluded on 23 June, when the jury returned a verdict of not guilty by reason of insanity. This was despite Toppan's efforts to appear sane during the trial. She was hoping that if she was found guilty, she might have a chance at eventually being released from prison. Toppan was only 48 years old at the time, and delusionally believed that the court would not give her a life sentence, despite having confessed and acknowledged that she was a cold-blooded murderer in open court.

During the trial, Toppan told the jury that she was sane, with her reasoning being that she knew committing murder was wrong, but did it anyway. In her mind, if she was insane, she wouldn't have been able to understand that killing was a crime. Counter to her arguments (or perhaps because of them), the jury deemed her to be insane, and she was committed to the Taunton Insane Hospital in Taunton, Massachusetts, for the remainder of her life.

Aftermath

Toppan remained confined to Taunton Insane Hospital until she died on 17 August 1938. At the time of her death, she was 84 years old and in poor health—the exact type of person she'd spent her professional career preying upon. While she came from a terrible background and suffered enormous hardships early in her life, Toppan never seemed to recognize the advantages she possessed that could have allowed her to live a long, happy, and fruitful existence. Unlike her siblings, she was smart and able to hold down a respectable job, while people cared enough about her to help her in many ways.

Without the support of the Toppan family, she would never have been able to secure a career as a nurse, and even after getting fired from Massachusetts General, the administration at Cambridge liked her so much that they hired her to return there. Even her private patients and their families overlooked numerous transgressions due to their belief that she provided high-quality care, and it was only after going overboard and murdering an entire family that resulted in the full breadth of her crimes finally coming to light. Toppan proved that she was her own worst enemy, and there was nobody to blame for her downfall other than herself.

Chapter 5

Stephan Letter

Widely considered at the time of his arrest to be Germany's most deadly mass murderer since World War II, Stephan Letter spent a year and a half terrorizing the Bavarian town of Sonthofen with a series of horrific serial killings. Most of his victims were over the age of 75, which helped him to disguise his murders as deaths resulting from natural causes. By some estimates, he murdered more than 29 people, all within the timespan of January 2003 to July 2004. His is a case study in how childhood trauma can cause permanently stunted development in a person, leading to fatal results for those around them.

Background and Family

Stephan Letter was born on 17 September 1978 in Herdecke, North Rhine-Westphalia, Germany. His father was a bookkeeper, and his mother was a homemaker, but they divorced while Letter was still very young. He was left in his mother's custody, which proved to be disastrous for the boy. Without his father around to mitigate the damage caused by his mother's severe mental illnesses, all of her negative attention was focused on her son. She seemed determined to use him to satisfy her own compulsions, and he later accused her of traumatic physical, psychological, and emotional abuse.

Upbringing

Letter's mother supposedly inflicted significant psychological damage upon him throughout his childhood. She repeatedly told him and others that he was "slow" and "dimwitted." His mother did everything in her power to undermine his confidence and make him feel like he was worthless. There were many instances where she forced him to visit psychologists, demanding that they diagnose him with some sort of mental or learning disability. The doctors failed to give the results she desired, and she would simply move on to the next, subjecting her son to a battery of unnecessary testing.

It was believed that Letter's mother suffered from Munchausen Syndrome by proxy (MSP), deliberately causing him to become ill in order to garner sympathy from others. She allegedly used a variety of poisons and drugs to keep her son in a near-constant state of poor health, while at the same time, gaslighting him into believing he was mentally challenged. His mother basked in the attention she received for her "strength" and "perseverance" in dealing with such a sickly, difficult child. Nobody stepped in to alleviate Letter's suffering at his mother's hands, which had an enormous effect on how he viewed the world later in life.

He became aware early on in his childhood that his mother's behavior and actions weren't normal. When

Letter was around 7 years old, he pleaded with his father to take him to school, not wanting to spend any more time with his mother than he already did. Every minute he was away from her represented a temporary relief from her constant belittling and gaslighting, as well as fewer opportunities for her to poison or drug him. However, his father stopped short of actually doing anything to save his son from the desperate situation in which the boy was trapped, not wanting to deal with the ticking time bomb of his ex-wife's mental illnesses.

Schooling

Letter received his early education in Herdecke, although he missed a fair amount of school due to his frequent illnesses. While he underperformed in his classes, this was primarily because of a lack of confidence in his intelligence and academic abilities. The trauma from his childhood resulted in him possessing a very conflicted mind. On the one hand, he had been told all his life by his mother that he wasn't smart or capable of doing well in school. On the other hand, he felt that his mental development wasn't stunted in the ways she insisted. Being a child, he was unable to grapple with the existential crisis that arose from his circumstances, and it manifested in his poor classroom performance.

While Letter's biggest aspiration growing up was to become a doctor, he did not achieve the grades needed to get accepted into medical school. Instead, he chose to enter a nursing career. During this time, he began dating a woman named Daniella, and the pair soon married. In addition to wanting to become a doctor, Letter also craved a normal domestic life and a happy relationship. He was in such a rush to get married that he failed to recognize the pre-existing problems in his relationship. Things didn't improve after they wed, and the marriage was difficult from the start. Both partners were riddled with mental scars from traumatic childhoods, and they were deeply codependent.

After finishing nursing school, Letter began his residency at the University Hospital Heidelberg in Ludwigsburg, Baden-Württemberg, Germany. He proved to be competent at his position, although the issues that eventually escalated to murder started there. Theft of medical supplies and drugs were the first problems that arose, but Letter managed to avoid detection until he departed from Heidelberg. Later on, the disappearance of supplies and several suspicious deaths were attributed to him, despite the lack of hard evidence due to the amount of time that had passed since the crimes were committed.

Professional Career

At the beginning of 2003, Letter got a job at the Sonthofen Clinic in Sonthofen, Germany, a small town nestled within the Bavarian Alps. Since the hospital specialized in geriatric care, it proved to be the ideal location for Letter to carry out his murder spree. He volunteered to work the night shift, which many of his co-workers believed was because he was ambitious, seeking to prove himself to further his professional career. While he was cordial with his colleagues, he was never particularly close with them, so they didn't see the kind of person he was in private. Anytime Daniella suggested inviting people from work over to the house, he demurred, insisting he'd rather spend time alone with her.

Letter once bragged to his wife about how he saved a patient's life by arriving just in time, insisting that if he'd gotten there 30 seconds later, they would've died. What he didn't tell her was that this was a game he played, toying with his patients' lives. Wanting to feel powerful and in control over life and death, he would sometimes administer drugs to patients for the specific purpose of coming in at the last minute to "save" them. This satisfied his disturbing compulsions while also making him look like an extremely talented nurse to his colleagues and superiors.

By "proving" his skills, he was given increased responsibilities with less oversight. It was a simple matter for him to kill his victims when nobody else was watching him. At the same time, the fact that he had gotten away with stealing drugs for so long emboldened him. He didn't think anyone would notice the missing medications because he never saw any indication that the hospital was on high alert. Even Daniella questioned if he was nervous that he'd be caught, but he brushed her concerns off, asserting that he was being careful and not taking enough to cause suspicion. What he didn't tell her was that he was also using the stolen medications to commit murder.

Murders

Letter's preference for working the night shift was motivated by the lack of other staff on duty, which offered him the freedom to carry out his murders unabated. He targeted elderly and infirm patients, which meant that the deaths of his victims didn't immediately raise any alarms. Letter was very clever and methodical in the way he killed patients, sedating them first to prevent them from making a fuss. After dosing them with the sedative, he administered the muscle relaxant known as succinylcholine. This made it appear that his victims had passed away from complications related to their poor health rather than murder.

During Letter's tenure at the Sonthofen Clinic, 80 patients died while he was working his nursing shifts. The majority of his victims were aged 75 or older, with his oldest victim being 94 years old, but he also killed patients as young as 40 years old. It wasn't unusual for old or sick patients to die, and Letter generally performed well in his duties, which helped him avoid suspicion in the beginning. The murders were written off as typical deaths, at least until the body count continued to mount. Letter's ability to remain undetected diminished the more he killed. His behavior wasn't universally seen as harmless, and there was an increase in the number of people who questioned his motives.

By 2004, multiple patients were begging their families and other hospital workers not to be left alone with Letter. An elderly patient named Gertrud Reindl warned her family that someone in the hospital ward where she was being treated was trying to kill her. She focused her suspicions on Letter, but he did his best to assuage their fears and convince them that Gertrud was simply scared and paranoid. When she died soon after, her family reported her concerns to the administration, and they were far from the only source of negative feedback Letter was receiving.

Investigation and Capture

Medical supplies began disappearing at a worrisome rate from the Sonthofen Clinic throughout 2003 and 2004. At one point, ten vials of medications went missing from the hospital, and the administration put locks on the storage cabinets to prevent further thefts. Later, a large amount of sedatives, anesthetics, and muscle relaxants disappeared, and Letter was among the few people with regular access to the drugs. A colleague followed him and discovered him in the room from which the drugs were being stolen, and the stockpile was found to be depleted shortly after. In order to prove Letter was the culprit, the hospital set a trap for him, hoping to catch him red-handed.

Prior to and following the night shift, when Letter often worked, the stock of medications was checked, where it was determined the drugs were definitively stolen. The medications could only be taken out with the written authorization of a doctor, and no such authorization existed. A check of the rotation duty roster showed that Letter was on staff every time the drugs disappeared. At the time, the fear was that he was stealing the drugs for personal use or to sell; they never anticipated that he was murdering patients with the hospital's own medical supplies.

A fellow nurse witnessed Letter stealing drugs and alerted the hospital administration. By this point, they had enough evidence to contact the police, and Letter was arrested on 29 July 2004. While in custody, Letter shocked the officers by not only confessing to the thefts, but also to countless murders. However, he immediately attempted to frame the killings as "mercy," insisting that he only did it to ease the suffering of his patients in a way that nobody was willing to do for him. This was a controversial position to take, since the memory of Nazi experiments with euthanasia remains a stain on the public consciousness in Germany.

Motivation

Letter prided himself on becoming a professional nurse, viewing it as a significant achievement after spending his childhood being told by his mother that he wasn't smart enough to amount to anything. However, he also hated the patients under his care, as he saw himself reflected in them. They were sick and unable to help themselves, just like he was when he was stuck being abused by his mother. He also hated people in general for the failure of everyone around him to save him from his childhood trauma. This made it all too easy for him to justify committing murder on a massive scale.

Due to a combination of his childhood and professional experiences, Letter saw drugs as a catch-all solution to all health-related ailments. However, his perspective was twisted, and the manner in which he chose to administer his personal brand of "treatment" frequently led to more pain and suffering. Letter wasn't trained as a doctor, so he didn't possess the knowledge that comes with the extensive training doctors must undergo to receive their medical license. Yet he often felt like he knew better than licensed professionals. In addition to his arrogance, he also had a habit of flouting hospital regulations by treating patients in ways he wasn't authorized.

During one incident, a 22-year-old soldier was admitted into the hospital for minor injuries sustained in a fall, and the injections Letter gave her caused her to lose consciousness. She later recovered, but he should have never administered drugs to her in the first place, only doing so because he believed they would help, despite those with the proper medical training understanding it was an inappropriate solution. These types of actions were a result of lingering feelings of inadequacy that stemmed from Letter's childhood. He wanted to be a doctor, and his failure to succeed in that aspiration made him determined to prove he could do the job of doctors, regardless of his lack of formal training.

Daniella suffered from her own psychological problems, having been sexually abused by a family member when she was younger. Letter later felt frustrated by her inability to provide him with the intimate relationship he'd hoped for. According to him, she often recoiled at his touch, and rarely agreed to have sex with him. This was his excuse as to why he began stealing drugs from the hospital—he sought to treat her issues with the medications in order to help her get over her anxiety in the bedroom. Daniella's inability to push past her mental problems angered Letter, and he resented the fact that he viewed her as unwilling to seek professional treatment. His frustration was taken out on his victims, whose fate he could control in a way he couldn't with his wife at home.

Trial

In November 2004, while Letter was still awaiting trial, the prosecution grappled with how to charge him. They initially believed his story about being an "angel of mercy," and through his lawyer, he insisted that he "wanted to liberate their souls." According to Letter, he viewed his patients as being "trapped in their sick bodies." When the prosecution announced they would seek manslaughter charges, it upset many people, especially the families of his victims. Petra Reindl, the daughter of Gertrud, told the media, "Letter should be charged with murder, not manslaughter. He was trying to play God by deciding whether patients should live or die."

During this period, there were ongoing exhumations on the remains of more possible victims. The authorities were investigating 40 patients who died in a similar manner to Letter's victims, while another 38 patients were already cremated, so they could not be used as evidence. After a portion of the exhumed bodies were found to have been killed via succinylcholine poisoning, a search conducted on Letter's home uncovered unsealed vials of the drug that were traced back to the Sonthofen Clinic. This was enough to upgrade some of the charges against Letter from manslaughter to murder.

When the trial itself finally commenced in February 2006, he was formally charged with the deaths of 28 patients—12 counts of murder, 15 counts of manslaughter, and 1 count of killing on request. The prosecution handily dismantled Letter's defense team's claims that he only killed his victims to spare them from the agony of a slow, painful death. It turned out that he wasn't even the nurse assigned to care for multiple victims, with some in stable condition and being prepared for discharge when they died.

After a nine-month trial, the end came in November 2006. Letter was found guilty on all counts with which he was charged. Harry Rechner, the judge presiding over the trial, sentenced Letter to life imprisonment. In an unusual move under German law, he further declared that there should be no upper limit placed on the sentence, preventing Letter from having the chance for release after 15 years in accordance with good behavior. When the verdict was read, Letter—only 28 years old at the time—lost all the color in his face and mouthed the words "I'm sorry" to his lawyer.

Aftermath

Letter's life sentence resulted in his confinement within the prison facility in Straubing, Germany. Until the discovery of the serial killings committed by Neils Högel in 2006, Letter was considered to have murdered more people than anyone since the Nazi regime during the Second World War. Daniella never formally filed for divorce from her husband, but records indicate she has only visited him intermittently over the years since his incarceration began. He remains in prison to this day, with no hope of ever breathing air as a free man again for the rest of his life.

Chapter 6

Arnfinn Nesset

Arnfinn Nesset is a Norwegian registered nurse and serial killer who operated in the early 1980s. His obsession with death led him to make the move from a healer of the sick to a taker of lives. The most disturbing aspect of Nesset's murders is the fact that he is able to walk around a free man for almost two decades. While he once claimed to have killed as many as 138 victims, he was never properly punished for his crimes. He was in charge of helpless individuals who relied on him to provide the care and support necessary to keep them alive; instead, he robbed them of that life while they could do nothing to stop him. In the case of Nesset, justice was never properly served. The system failed to protect his victims, and it failed to punish their killer.

Background and Family

Arnfinn Nesset was born on 25 October 1936 in Stjørna, Sør-Trøndelag, Norway, to unmarried parents. His mother was single at the time, and his father was a one-night stand who had no interest in raising a child or being involved in his son's life. Nesset never met his father, while his mother worked a series of odd jobs and relied on her parents' income to provide the necessities for her child. Her family wasn't particularly religious, but they were very traditional, and they felt ashamed that their young daughter had gotten pregnant without being married. They did their best to avoid allowing outsiders to know the truth, although they stopped short from outright claiming Nesset to be their son instead of their grandson.

Upbringing

Nesset was raised in the childhood home of his mother, who required her family's assistance to care for her young son. As a boy, he was considered quiet and shy, rarely leaving the house or going out with friends. He felt resentment toward his mother, who he blamed for the rejection of his father, and let those emotions broil within him for years as he grew up. Due to his taciturn nature, he never expressed his feelings to others, and they continued to build up, turning him into a pressure cooker. It was only a matter of time before something set him off, although rather than resulting in explosive anger, it manifested in cold, calculated cruelty.

Schooling

From 1st to 10th grade, Nesset attended the Åsly School in Rissa, Norway. His time there was uneventful, and while he was by no means an excellent student, he always managed to pass his classes. Completing his education there, he moved on to the nearby Johan Bojer

High School, where again, his academic performance was acceptable but not exceptional. Graduating in 1954, he moved to Trondheim, attending nursing school at what is now a part of Sør-Trøndelag University College. The school was located in the neighborhood of Øya in Trondheim. After acquiring his nursing degree, he began seeking work professionally as a registered nurse in the Sør-Trøndelag region.

During Nesset's school days, he developed a worrying fascination with death. Classmates from Åsly recalled an incident where a cat got hit by a vehicle near the school, and he sat down to watch it for over an hour as it died a slow, painful death. For the next few days, he spoke of nothing else but the excitement it brought him to witness the last vestiges of life literally slip away from a living creature. He claimed to have been able to tell the very moment when it succumbed to its injuries because he could "feel" its soul depart from its body. This was the earliest known incident of Nesset becoming enamored with the concepts of life and death.

Professional Career

The first professional nursing job Nesset got was at a clinic in Ørland around 1958. He found that he didn't like treating the younger patients and began seeking work in elderly care. Even before he began killing people, he enjoyed experiencing the deaths of patients when they perished from natural causes. When older patients appeared to be nearing the end, he started spending an inordinate amount of time attending to them, hoping to be present at the moment when they died. Others merely thought he was being kind, offering comfort to those closing in on their final breath. This helped him advance his career and earned the trust of his superiors.

Nesset was hired at the Orkdal Nursing Home, a geriatric care facility in Orkdal, Norway, in 1962. He proved to be very competent at his job and even showed a knack for handling administrative duties. Over the next decade and a half, he embedded himself within the nursing home's day-to-day operations, becoming an important piece in the machinery running the place. In August 1977, Nesset was promoted to the position of director at the facility. With his new status running the nursing home, he had more freedom than ever before to act in whatever manner he pleased. He had the trust of the administration, the staff, and the patients, allowing him to get away with many crimes in the ensuing years.

Murders

The unhealthy fixation Nesset held when it came to death was initially sated by simply observing elderly patients passing away while he was on duty. However, he craved to have a more direct hand in helping unfortunate souls "shuffle off this mortal coil." His experience as a registered nurse allowed him access to the necessary tools to perform his ghastly murders, but there weren't any ample opportunities to kill without getting caught. He needed to have patience before he got the chance to murder patients. In the meantime, he watched and waited, studying the types of methods that might let him get away with murder while plotting the best way to enjoy the experience when he finally pulled the trigger.

For much of his tenure at Orkdal Nursing Home, Nesset committed a series of crimes from which he benefited financially. He forged legal documents such as patient records and wills, as well as embezzled money from the facility where he worked. Despite taking great risks to carry out these crimes, Nesset never appeared to take advantage of the wealth he acquired. He wasn't known for wearing expensive clothes or driving flashy cars, and his home was quite modest. It seemed that his motive was to experience the thrill of successfully executing the crimes far more than any material rewards. His desire for emotional satisfaction above practical results was also evident in his murders. He never killed for revenge or personal gain, only to enjoy wielding power over other people, particularly when it came to life and death.

Beginning in 1978, Nesset decided that he'd accrued enough of a positive reputation as the director of the nursing home to avoid suspicion when he finally carried out his plans. His weapon of choice was the anesthetic known as succinylcholine, which caused paralysis in the muscles. This immobilized his victims, preventing them from getting help as they died. He also administered the drug in such high doses that it quickly proved fatal. The rapidity with which his victims perished meant he could remain present and watch the light fade from their eyes, satisfying his long-held ambitions of taking human lives.

The sudden surge in suspicious deaths at Nesset's facility didn't go unnoticed. While nobody working at the nursing home seemed to find it odd since they were around sick and dying people every day, journalists caught wind of the alarming rate at which patients dropped dead and began to investigate. They started digging into the matter in 1981, and their attention soon fell upon Nesset. The suspicious deaths ramped up during his time serving as director, and the journalists found it unlikely that an administrator who regularly saw the actual statistics of patient deaths didn't see anything wrong with such a significant increase in the nursing home's average mortality rate.

Investigation and Capture

After the media investigation had gathered enough evidence, they turned their findings over to the police. It took the authorities two years and five months before they were ready to act on the information, arresting Nesset in 1982. His residence was searched, and a large quantity of succinylcholine was uncovered. Initially, he denied the accusations of murder and claimed he was using the drug to poison a pack of stray dogs that kept damaging his property. According to him, they would show up at night, dig through his yard, and toss his trash all over the place. However, there were no records of anyone in the area contacting animal control about the stray dogs, as well as no evidence as to how Nesset disposed of their corpses.

Following further interrogation, he confessed that he didn't use the drugs to kill stray dogs but to murder his own patients at the nursing home. During his first confession, he alleged to have killed 27 victims over about 20 years, beginning all the way back in 1962. In the next round of interrogation, he increased the number of victims to 46, and later 72. With his final confession, he told the police that he'd murdered 138 victims, but his body count was so high, he couldn't remember all of their identities. According to him, the murders occurred at three different healthcare facilities, and he did not have a preference as to the ages of his victims.

When it came time to charge Nesset, the police could not find evidence for many of the murders he claimed were committed at the other medical institutions. They limited the scope of his charges to 25 counts of murder, as well as multiple counts of attempted murder, embezzlement, and forgery. All the victims he was charged with killing happened at Orkdal Nursing Home between the years of 1981 and 1982. However, just before the commencement of his trial, he suddenly recanted all his confessions, once again maintaining he was innocent of murder.

Motivation

The primary reason for Nesset's murder spree was control. He wanted to control how his victims lived and how they died. Getting to watch them die provided him with a thrill he couldn't get anywhere else, and he was perfectly positioned to carry out his sick fantasies. Nesset also prided himself on self-control, managing to keep his dark impulses in check for much of his career. Unfortunately, the moment he decided to commit his first murder, he lost that aspect of himself. Unable to control his actions any longer, he killed so many patients in such a short span of time that outside observers couldn't help but take notice. If he had displayed the same amount of self-control after he started murdering his victims as he did before, there's a good chance he would have never been caught.

Trial

In preparation for the trial, the authorities had four independent psychiatrists perform assessments on Nesset to determine if he was competent to stand before the court. They all came to the same conclusion: the defendant was legally sane. Nesset's trial began in October 1982, and pleaded not guilty to the charges against him. In spite of the psychiatric examination results, his defense team attempted to portray him as mentally ill. The success he enjoyed during his long career as a registered nurse and nursing home administrator ended up hurting his case. It was determined to be unbelievable that someone who couldn't tell the difference between right and wrong would have lasted as long as they did as a professional caregiver, even if he was feigning concern for his patients the entire time.

Ultimately, the defense team's tactics failed, and on 13 March 1983, the court found Nesset guilty on 22 of the 25 counts of murder. He was also found guilty on 1 count of attempted murder and stealing $1,800 from 5 of his victims. The court sentenced him to 21 years imprisonment, which was the maximum sentence allowable by Norwegian law at the time. After the sentence expired, he was to undergo another 10 years of preventative detention. He was only 46 years old at the time of his conviction, and was set to be released in 2004, at the age of 67.

Aftermath

Nesset was released from prison after only serving 12 of his 21-year sentence. He was reportedly paroled early due to good behavior. This was followed by 10 years of supervised release, which ended in 2005, only one year later than his original date of parole. Because of this, Nesset ended up regaining his complete freedom 9 years prior to the 2014 date initially recommended by the court. Once he had finished serving his sentence, he changed his name and moved to an undisclosed location in order to hide from the piercing gaze of the general public. As of 2023, he remains alive, celebrating his 87th birthday on 25 October. Owing to the lenient sentencing guidelines in Norway, Nesset only spent about six months in prison for each count of murder on which he was convicted.

Chapter 7

Roger Andermatt

Roger Andermatt was an assistant nurse and serial killer from Switzerland who was known as "The Death-Keeper of Lucerne." Racking up a body count of at least 22 victims, he is still considered the most prolific serial killer in Swiss history to this day. The number of deaths for which he was directly responsible was, at minimum, twice as many as Michel Peiry, who was Switzerland's previous record holder for serial killings. Peiry had between 5 and 11 victims, which was dwarfed by the horrific death toll amassed by Andermatt.

Background and Family

Roger Andermatt was born on 14 May 1969 in Lucerne, Switzerland, to Henry and Emma Andermatt (née Meyer). Henry worked primarily as a banking agent, while Emma worked as a schoolteacher. Andermatt's parents had relationship problems well before he was born, and their constant fighting only got worse after he arrived. The family was known in the neighborhood for the loud arguments that could be heard by passersby, and on several occasions, the police were called in by concerned witnesses who feared possible domestic abuse. However, there was no evidence that the confrontations between Henry and Emma ever got physical.

Henry was likely an alcoholic, considering he spent an inordinate amount of time in pubs or with a drink glued to his hand. Emma displayed hints of having a mental illness—possibly narcissistic personality disorder—but was never officially diagnosed. She had the tell-tale symptoms, including an obsession with praise, a high degree of self-importance, and very fragile self-esteem. She never took criticism well, which contributed to the fights with her husband. He always knew exactly what to say in order to chip away at her armor and jab her with whatever words would cut her the deepest.

Upbringing

Shortly after Andermatt's birth, his parents had an explosive row when Henry chose to stay out all night drinking rather than return home to help his wife care for their newborn baby. Emma threatened to take their son and leave, resulting in Henry accusing her of infidelity. He questioned Andermatt's "true" parentage, although he never pursued the matter further, indicating that it was simply a tactic to rile Emma in the midst of their battle. On the other hand, Andermatt recalled his mother often inviting men from the neighborhood over when her school was on break, and his father was at work. He later assumed she was carrying on affairs but never received confirmation.

The arguments between Henry and Emma would sometimes get so bad that the young Andermatt was forced to hide in his bedroom closet and wear earmuffs to block out the yelling. He was riddled with anxiety as a child, and the sound of raised voices always seemed to make him nervous. While Henry and Emma never became physically abusive, the emotional and psychological toll it took on their son was undeniable. It became clear that the toxicity of their relationship was not just harming themselves but Andermatt as well. This finally convinced them that the best thing they could do for their family was to split up.

Andermatt's parents divorced around 1980, and he moved with his mother to Germany. She was able to get a teaching job in the suburbs outside the city of Freiburg, which was close to the Switzerland border and had a sizable Swiss population. Andermatt wasn't a huge fan of Germany, though, and spent most of his time there feeling homesick. He didn't make friends easily, owing to his anxious nature, and his dislike of the area prevented him from going out much. As soon as he got a chance to return to Switzerland, he took it, leaving his mother and Germany behind.

Schooling

The earliest days of Andermatt's education occurred in Lucerne until his parents' divorce necessitated the move to Germany. He attended the same school where his mother taught until he entered high school. During his time as a student, he fared poorly but managed to at least pass his classes with high enough grades to avoid being held back. Andermatt wasn't particularly intelligent, although his poor performance in school might have also been linked to his anxiety. He also didn't get along with his classmates, who often bullied him for being "the weird kid."

After graduating from high school, Andermatt was unsure what to do with his life. He wasn't qualified to go to university, but he rejected the idea of working in a minimum wage job. By 1990, he'd had enough of living in Germany, blaming his surroundings for his lack of prospects, and decided to move back to Lucerne. Following the move, he took nursing classes, and while he never got a professional certification, the experience helped him get a position as an assistant nurse in a local clinic.

Professional Career

Andermatt began his professional career working at a health clinic in Lucerne. In 1995, he got a job at a nearby nursing home known as Eichhof, which brought him into contact with elderly and infirm patients. He also served as an assistant nurse at other nursing homes affiliated with Eichhof, moving between them to help out when they were short-staffed. One facility that cared for invalids was located in the town of Sarnen, which is about 12 miles south of Lucerne. He wasn't necessarily great at his job, but the lack of viable candidates and an overflow of patients in need of care meant that the facilities that employed him didn't have the luxury of replacing him with someone more competent.

In his spare time, Andermatt worked as a dance instructor at a local studio in Lucerne. He also indulged in a career as an amateur DJ, operating under the name "Ro

Gee." However, he rarely performed at any gigs, and most of his work was creating poorly-done remixes of popular EDM and rap songs that he uploaded to the internet. Caregiving was never a passion for Andermatt—just something he could do to make money and pass the time. If he had been smarter or more talented, he would have pursued other avenues of employment.

Murders

Between 1995 and 2001, Andermatt murdered at least 22 victims. According to his confessions, he might have killed even more, with him admitting to 27 murders. His favorite method of killing his victims was to inject them with a tranquilizer, and then smother them with a plastic bag or cloth towels. The majority of his victims ranged from ages 66 to 95. Many of his victims weren't actually dying, and their condition varied between chronically ill to old, but otherwise healthy. Some of the patients were experiencing symptoms of Alzheimer's Disease and required additional care, yet they were hardly knocking on death's door. This made his insistence that he wasn't killing for personal reasons ring false.

The tranquilizers administered to his victims kept them docile, but they were likely fully aware of what was happening to them when he suffocated them. Because asphyxiation results in cutting off the oxygen supply to the brain, it is a horrible way to die, and Andermatt's victims would have suffered immensely, not to mention the anguish of realizing they were going to die and there was nothing they could do about it. Anyone purporting to seek to euthanize patients to ease their pain would choose a painless method to enact death. Andermatt either didn't care enough to understand how asphyxiation works, or he knew and simply didn't care.

Investigation and Capture

In early 2001, the families of patients who died in Eichhof and other nursing homes in Lucerne grew suspicious about the manner in which their loved ones had been treated. Most of Andermatt's victims were women, and while elderly patients dying isn't unusual, the amount of sudden, unexplainable deaths brought up questions that needed more satisfying answers. The police got involved and exhumed the bodies of Andermatt's victims. Autopsies revealed that they had been drugged and suffocated, which indicated that they'd been murdered. Andermatt had falsified medical records to cover up his crimes, which itself is a crime.

After the authorities felt that they'd gathered enough evidence against Andermatt, they arrested him in June 2001. Following three months of interrogations and investigations, he finally confessed to having committed 27 murders. At first, he only claimed to have killed 9 victims, but later admitted to another 18 murders. He also told the police about several other crimes he committed, such as attempting but failing to murder 5 elderly patients, forging medical records, and stealing money from his victims. His trial was set to begin in late 2004 or early 2005.

Motivation

Andermatt allegedly viewed himself as an "angel of mercy," murdering his victims to spare them from continuing to suffer the effects of aging or illness. At another point, he told investigators that the nursing homes where he worked were so overcrowded that it overwhelmed the staff to the point of being unable to provide quality care to anyone. By killing the older patients, it freed up the other caregivers to focus more attention on younger patients who had a better chance of living longer with the assistance of proper medical intervention.

There is a good chance that Andermatt inherited at least one mental illness in some form from his mother. He didn't suffer from narcissistic personality disorder, but he lived with a high degree of anxiety on a daily basis. The additional stress of working in such a busy and understaffed environment exacerbated his issues, and he eventually snapped. Killing elderly women entrusted to his care wasn't for the purpose of helping them, but helping himself. It eased his own burdens, as it meant a lighter workload and fewer patients to worry about. There was very little consideration given to others, as Andermatt was primarily concerned with how he was affected personally.

Trial

The authorities charged Andermatt with 22 counts of murder, 3 counts of attempted murder, and 2 counts of unfinished murder. The other 5 murders he confessed to committing were deemed assisted suicides, so he was not held responsible for those deaths. Andermatt stood trial to account for these crimes, and his defense team attempted to convince the court that he killed his victims out of sympathy, wishing to end their suffering. This tactic didn't work, and on 28 January 2005, he was convicted on all counts of murder, attempted murder, and unfinished murder.

At the close of the trial, the prosecutor had requested that Andermatt be sentenced to 17 years in prison. The judge, Rudolf Isenschmid, was so appalled by the defendant's actions that he chose to sentence him to life imprisonment. He told the court that the "victims were defenseless and that the convicted man had unscrupulously and insidiously abused their trust in the best care." Isenschmid didn't buy the defense argument that Andermatt was an "angel of mercy," instead viewing him as a cold-hearted serial killer. He was only 36 years old during his trial, which meant that he was set to spend a very long time in prison.

Aftermath

Andermatt appealed the court's decision to convict him, and the case was brought before the Lucerne High Court. On 15 February 2006, the court upheld the sentence of life imprisonment, but they convicted him for only 7 murders. The remaining 15 murders were reclassified as deliberate killings. Even with the reduced number of official murder victims, Andermatt was still convicted on more counts of murder than any other person in Swiss history. The court felt that because of how many victims he killed, he deserved to remain in prison for the rest of his life.

With the failure of his appeal, Andermatt resigned himself to his lot in life. As of 2023, he is 54 years old, and he is in relatively good health. He can look forward to many more years being stuck in prison, unable to hurt innocent victims ever again. Regardless of his assertions that he only killed due to compassion, he took the lives of patients who could have lived for at least several more years. The bottom line is that Andermatt got tired of putting in so much effort to care for needy patients, and his solution was to murder them when they were at their most vulnerable. He doesn't deserve to ever step foot outside the prison again.

Chapter 8

Ludivine Chambet

Ludivine Chambet was an unlicensed nursing assistant who became a serial killer after a significant personal loss. She became known as "The Poisoner of Chambéry" because of the method she chose to use to commit her murders. Chambet killed 10 victims, but had poisoned even more during the period when she was active. Her case is a strange one, because, unlike many other serial killers who operated in the medical field, she didn't seem to have any ulterior motives for the murders. From the beginning, she maintained the same excuse, and even psychiatrists who worked with her believed she was telling the truth—at least from her perspective.

Background and Family

Ludivine Chambet was born on 10 May 1983 in Chambéry, France, to Louis and Celine Chambet. Louis was a butcher who worked intermittently in shops around Chambéry, but was often unemployed. He struggled with alcoholism, and employers didn't feel like they could trust him to be both reliable and sober while handling dangerous butcher tools. Celine was a housekeeper, and her income kept the family afloat while her husband was looking for a job. This caused their marriage to be strained, and their issues spilled over into their relationship with their only child.

Chambet's birth was a difficult ordeal for Louis and Celine. She was born with a rare genetic disease known as Beckwith-Wiedemann Syndrome (BWS). This disease causes physical malformations in those who suffer from it. For Chambet, it manifested as an open abdomen, a very dangerous problem that could result in death if left untreated. The struggles her parents endured with her medical problems created additional stress for them, and they fought constantly. Louis blamed his wife for their daughter's physical deformities, while Celine saw it as a punishment from God for Louis' sins.

Upbringing

Chambet was raised in and around Chambéry, primarily in the small town of Challes-les-Eaux. Around the time she was born, Challes-les-Eaux only had a population of 2,580 residents. Due to her father's inability to keep a steady job, their family moved frequently, usually when they were forced to downsize. Chambet ended up in the middle of many of her parents' conflicts, and it had a negative effect on her psychological development. They tried to weaponize her against each other, and this twisted the way she viewed relationships, something she struggled with later in life.

When she was 8 years old, Chambet had to have surgery for tongue atrophy. An enlarged tongue is one of the symptoms of BWS, as is low blood sugar, which caused her to have frequent dizzy spells and fits of vomiting. Another way BWS affected her was with her balance, making it hard for her to participate in many physical activities with her peers. She suffered from low self-esteem, a consequence of her medical issues and the unrelenting teasing she received from those around her. According to Chambet, she was "especially teased at school," because people thought she was "tall, not beautiful."

Celine became an overbearing parent to her daughter, seeking to protect her and keep her safe. The way Chambet was treated by others upset Celine, and the way she chose to protect her child was by keeping her confined to their home. Chambet told psychiatrists, "I think it's safe to say she was overprotective of me because of my birth issues. I don't think we had cut the cord." However, Celine was also her biggest supporter, and she called her mother a "pillar." Without Celine, Chambet would have suffered even more ridicule and abuse during her childhood.

Unfortunately, Celine's anxiety rubbed off on her daughter, and Chambet exhibited similar signs of possessing the same issues. Chambet rarely participated in activities outside the home. As a teenager, she played basketball for a short time, but this ended when her knee gave out. She also attempted to play the accordion, taking private lessons from a local music teacher. However, Chambet gave up on the instrument after only a handful of lessons. For the most part, she didn't have any hobbies or interests. She spent her free time shopping with her mother.

In reference to the shopping trips Chambet would take with Celine, she said, "We went to see what's new, even if we didn't buy." During her childhood, Chambet's only real friend was her mother. Isolation and codependence transformed a normal mother-daughter bond into an unhealthy and toxic relationship. They spent an inordinate amount of time together, and Celine would unload her marital problems on her daughter. She resented Louis' inability to provide a stable life for them, and this perspective was passed down to Chambet. By the time the girl was 18 years old, she was on antidepressants to help with her severe anxiety and depression.

Schooling

Chambet possessed an average intelligence, and she was a fairly mediocre student in school. Most of her memories from her academic career involved teasing and bullying from her fellow students. She came to hate school and didn't wish to embark on a long educational journey. Instead of attending a local high school, she earned a Certificat d'Aptitude Professionnelle (CAP). The CAP program is designed to offer vocational qualifications that gives students access to a specific trade. Chambet received her CAP for tourism, but she also had aspirations to become a professional caregiver.

After earning her CAP, she entered a program to get a Brevet d'Etudes Professionelles (BEP). The BEP program is more demanding than the one for getting a CAP, and Chambet focused on health and social services. Following her successful completion of the program, she went on to become certified as a nursing assistant, being awarded a diploma upon finishing the nursing program. Once she had her nursing assistant certificate, she was able to fulfill her ambitions of becoming a professional caregiver.

Professional Career

It's important to note that Chambet's certification was not the same as a nursing license. She was considered an unlicensed nursing assistant (UAP), which meant that her caregiving duties required the oversight of a licensed practical nurse, registered nurse, or other healthcare professional. UAP's must prove their competence and skills before they're allowed to take on any duties involving direct patient treatment. At the start of her professional career, Chambet spent time moving between departments at a hospital in Jacob-Bellecombette, a commune in Savoie, France. During this time, she managed to gain the necessary experience to earn more responsibilities at her job.

Chambet transferred to the Établissement d'Hébergement pour Personnes Âgées Dépendantes (EHPAD), a nursing home in Chambéry. Around the same time, her mother was diagnosed with leukemia, and Chambet became her primary caregiver. Between her job and helping her mother, she didn't have time for romantic relationships. "It was not my primary goal to have a stable relationship with a man, to start a family," Chambet said. "My primary concern was my mother."

She was there every step of the way as the leukemia slowly ate away at her mother, leaving her in agony and suffering more with every day that passed. Celine only got worse, and there was nothing Chambet could do to stop it. Sadly, her mother succumbed to the disease on 27 June 2013. This left Chambet absolutely devastated. She later claimed that she saw her mother in the victims she murdered, and wanted to prevent them from suffering in the same manner. Dealing with Celine's illness, and eventually, the loss of her mother, was the trigger that caused Chambet to become a serial killer.

Murders

Chambet began murdering patients at EHPAD after her mother became very sick, killing her first victim in 2012. According to her, she saw a patient suffering in the same way as Celine and desired to ease that pain. Using sleeping pills, antipsychotics, and antidepressants that weren't prescribed by any doctors, Chambet injected the drug cocktail into her patient, hoping it would lessen the agonizing pain. However, she used too much of the drugs, and her patient ended up dying. To Chambet, this was an acceptable outcome because she equated death with a release from a sick and broken physical body.

Over the next year or two, Chambet murdered 9 more patients in a similar manner. In total, she killed 10 victims. The final one came on 27 November 2013, exactly five months after the death of her mother. She was treating a patient at EHPAD, and the woman suddenly fell into a coma and died. There didn't appear to be a logical reason for this to happen, so a toxicology examination was performed. They found the presence of drugs that nobody in the facility had prescribed, meaning the victim had been deliberately poisoned.

Investigation and Capture

Following the suspicious death of the EHPAD patient, the administration began looking back at previous deaths that occurred in the facility. They were horrified when they discovered that there were numerous other patients who died suddenly and without explanation. It soon became clear that there was someone murdering the patients at the nursing home. Nearly all the suspected victims were between the ages of 76 and 96. Many of the victims did not have any ailments that would have been fatal in the near future, so they could have continued to live longer if their lives hadn't been cut short.

The EHPAD administration checked the duty roster and compared the list of staff on duty at the times of the suspicious deaths. Almost all of them included the presence of Chambet, making her the prime suspect. Ultimately, it was determined that 13 patients had been poisoned in the same manner, and 10 of the poisoned victims died from the unauthorized drug cocktails. The administrators contacted the police, and on 10 December 2013, Chambet was quickly arrested. However, her family didn't believe the accusations against her. They insisted that she was "simple, kind and generous."

Motivation

Chambet never had a normal life. She was tormented because of her physical ailments as a child, and she lacked any sort of social life outside of the home. Her relationship with her overprotective mother made her fragile and unable to handle typical interactions with other people. Even at work, she was usually overlooked by her peers. They never noticed how her behavior changed after Celine's death, because they never got to know her beforehand. Following her mother's death, Chambet would suddenly scream or cry for no reason in the halls of the nursing home, and still, nobody seemed to care enough to find out what was going on with her.

The ostracization Chambet experienced in conjunction with the loss of her beloved mother, set her on a path to murder. She didn't see killing her victims as a horrible tragedy. In her mind, she was doing the right thing by ending their pain and suffering. Chambet didn't want others to go through what Celine was forced to endure. "It's mom's suffering that I modeled on these people," she told the authorities. It seemed like she truly didn't understand why her actions were considered unacceptable in a civilized society. Unlike many of her contemporaries who murdered their own patients and tried to claim they were an "angel of mercy," Chambet genuinely believed she was helping her victims when she killed them.

Trial

Ten counts of murder and three counts of attempted murder were included in Chambet's indictment. The court eventually heard her case after nearly four years of waiting. The trial started on May 23, 2017, and Chambet's caregiving activities came under investigation. The prosecution made an effort to portray her as a cold-blooded, ruthless killer who was incapable of feeling empathy. "It wasn't about euthanasia, since the retirement home wasn't a deathbed, and Ludivine Chambet knew exactly what she was doing when she gave her drug cocktails," they claimed. They intended to persuade the court that Chambet wasn't attempting to alleviate anyone's pain in this way.

The prosecutor further admonished her, saying, "She dares to say that she did not want to kill them, and just wanted to appease them. But Ludivine Chambet is dangerous, even with her little girlish ways. The horror of the case is indisputable. These are serial murders." This perspective was not shared by everyone involved in the case, though. The psychiatrists who examined her believed that Ludivine Chambet's impassivity was contrary to a "murderous nature," and it actually showed "the fragility and psychic immaturity of her mind." The conflict between psychological experts and the prosecution caused some confusion about the culpability of Chambet.

The defense team countered this by pushing the "angel of mercy" angle, which included Chambet herself speaking on her own behalf. She continuously insisted that she simply wanted to "relieve them, soothe them," in regard to her victims. She also claimed that her mind was "mixed, overturned, turned upside down." During the trial, she tried to make the jury understand the reasoning behind her actions, but after a brief period where she could recall the events that took place, she would end up blacking out, unable to remember anything.

The trial only lasted two weeks, and the jury took six hours to deliberate the case. The Advocate General had recommended a sentence of 30 years imprisonment.

The jury returned a verdict of guilty on all counts. They explained that they believed she was responsible for the murders, since she knowingly administered psychotropic drugs to the victims and was well aware of what effect that would have on them. Chambet was given 25 years imprisonment, which upset the families of her victims, considering it was even less time than was recommended. However, she was also given 10 years in a psychiatric ward following her release.

Aftermath

Immediately after the verdict was handed down, Chambet had her medical certification revoked. She was consigned to prison and forced to have regular meetings with psychiatrists. They were impressed by her attitude and willingness to work on fixing the issues that had hounded her for the entirety of her life. One of her psychiatrists revealed, "She is trying to understand her actions, and it is a long process." He also claimed, "She is eager to appear, take responsibility, and speak to the families, but she will only be able to do so to the best of her ability. She will only have to offer what she has discovered about herself. We hope that his message will be heard and understood."

While in prison, Chambet finally picked up a regular hobby: reading. She was noted as spending much of her free time in the prison library. Her favorite genre of books are romance novels, but she also picked up a few books about mother-daughter relationships. With the aid of her psychiatrists, Chambet has finally accepted that her relationship with Celine was not healthy, and she wants to learn more about what a non-toxic parental relationship should look like.

As of 2023, Chambet is 40 years old, and has only served a little over 6 years of her sentence. She will be released in 2042, at which point she will be 59 years old, and still looking at 10 years in a psychiatric ward. Chambet won't have completely served out her sentence until 2052, and she will be 69 years old. It's unlikely she'll get the chance to enjoy her freedom for very long, especially if she needs the help of a caregiver. For her sake, hopefully her nurse doesn't offer the same "mercy" that she gave to her victims.

Chapter 9

Lucy Letby

Lucy Letby is a former neonatal nurse and British serial killer whose murders spanned an entire year, from June 2015 to June 2016. She is an enigma when it comes to serial killers, as her background doesn't fit the typical profile of those who commit mass murder. There were no obvious warning signs, and her killing spree appeared to come out of nowhere. As far as anyone knows, there was nothing that triggered it. Letby seemingly woke up one day and decided to start murdering infants. Due to the fact that her victims were all babies, she is considered the most prolific serial killer of children.

Background and Family

Lucy Letby was born on 4 January 1990 in Hereford, England, to John and Susan Letby. John worked as a furniture retail manager, and Susan was an accounts clerk. There was a significant age gap between the couple—John was 14 years older than Susan. They both wanted children but struggled to conceive. When Susan finally got pregnant, they were elated, but their new baby had a difficult birth. If it wasn't for the nurses at the hospital where Letby was born, she very well could have died shortly after taking her first breath. At the time of Letby's birth, John was 44 years old, while Susan was 30 years old.

Upbringing

Letby's childhood was relatively normal. Unlike many other serial killers, she didn't suffer from abuse. This makes it hard to trace exactly what caused her to become a murderer. From all accounts, Letby was a happy child and had plenty of friends. She wasn't a loner, she wasn't bullied or rejected by her peers, and she never had any traumatic experiences. Friends described her as "quite awkward and giddy." Her safe and pleasant upbringing caused a bizarre disconnect when examining her later actions. It indicates that when it comes to Letby, it's a case of nature versus nurture where her dark nature won out.

Schooling

From the ages of 11 to 16, Letby went to Aylestone School in Hereford. It was also the same school where Rachel Whitear was a student before her heroin overdose that initiated a serious anti-drug campaign throughout the United Kingdom. Letby was a decent student, but fairly unexceptional. She didn't stand out from the hundreds of other students being educated there at the time.

After leaving Aylestone, Letby enrolled at Hereford Sixth Form College, which was also located in Herefordshire. It was for students between the ages of 16 and 19.. Letby performed well enough there that she had the opportunity to attend university. She was the first person in her family to do so, and her parents were exceedingly proud of this accomplishment.

For a brief period prior to leaving for university, Letby had a part time job at the WHSmith in High Town, Hereford. She chose to go to the University of Chester, pursuing a degree in nursing. Recalling the stories about her troubled birth and the nurses who valiantly saved her life, Letby had long harbored aspirations to become a professional caregiver. While working on getting her nursing degree, she was placed at Liverpool Women's Hospital and the Countess of Chester Hospital as a student nurse, helping her gain valuable on-the-job experience.

When Letby graduated from university in September 2011, her parents were elated. They put a notice in the local newspaper to celebrate their daughter's graduation. It read: "Letby, Lucy - BSc Hons in Child Nursing. We are so proud of you after all your hard work. Love Mum and Dad." They continued to be as supportive of her dreams as they'd always been, and never tried to steer her in a different direction. In fact, they were more than willing to pay for her education, and doted on her constantly. She was their only child, and they wished to maintain a close relationship with her.

Professional Career

In 2012, Letby was placed at Liverpool Women's Hospital for training. She did well enough to continue on to a proper nursing career. Her first job after university was in 2012 when she was hired as a registered nurse in the neonatal unit at the Countess of Chester Hospital. She appeared to thrive in the position, taking her duties seriously and serving as a source of comfort for the families of the patients by interacting with them in a positive way.

Her responsibilities included caring for babies with many different needs and levels of support. According to her, she enjoyed witnessing the children making progress toward better health and helping to support their families. The patients' families have said that she was always happy to chat about her life. She would even speak about the fact that she was single and didn't regret her current relationship status.

By 2013, Letby was firmly entrenched in the hospital's culture and became involved in many of their causes. She was a major participant in a fundraising campaign to gather funds for a new neonatal unit. Due to her amiable demeanor, she had plenty of friends and a good relationship with her colleagues. Anytime a baby under her care died from what appeared to be underlying health conditions, her fellow nurses showered her with support, as she seemed to take the losses very hard.

Letby returned to Liverpool Women's Hospital in early 2015 for additional nursing training. While questions had been floated about her competency due to the inordinate number of deaths amongst the babies under her supervision, she had earned the full support of the hospital administration. They wanted to increase her responsibilities, and following her training, she returned to the Countess of Chester Hospital, having now qualified for work with babies requiring intensive care. This placed her in charge of patients who were already in serious danger of dying.

However, while the administration loved Letby, doctors who worked on the ward were convinced she was more responsible for the deaths than she claimed. Their grievances against her were mostly ignored, and when rumors began to spread that Letby was killing patients on purpose, she successfully convinced the administrators that the doctors were wrongly accusing her of wrongdoing. She was given an apology by the hospital trust, as well as assurances that the doctors responsible would be "dealt with."

In addition, the administration was ready to offer her a place at the prestigious Alder Hey Children's Hospital in Liverpool, England, as well as support to either undergo advanced nurse training or earn a master's degree. This action was delayed, though, as the conflict between Letby and the doctors ramped up. Hoping to protect Letby, the administration transferred her from the night shift to the day shift in April 2016. Three months later, she was moved to the patient experience team. Later, she was transferred again, this time to the risk and patient safety office. It was when Letby was working there when she got arrested.

Murders

It's likely that Letby was responsible for numerous infant deaths throughout her career as a result of neglect and incompetent care, but none of them could be undisputedly linked to her. She didn't start committing the murders until her return to the Countess of Chester Hospital following her second training stint, killing her first victim on 8 June 2015. The victim, only identified as Child A, was born six weeks premature alongside his twin sister, Child B. Child A was stable and healthy when he was placed in Letby's care, only several days old. His health rapidly deteriorated over the next half hour, and an hour later, he was dead. Letby injected air into his IV, causing a pulmonary embolism.

Child B, the twin sister of Child A, was Letby's next target, with the attack spanning from 8 June to 11 June 2015. As with her first victim, she used an injection of air into Child B's IV. This occurred only 28 hours after Child A's death. However, unlike her twin brother, Child B was resuscitated after suffering an embolism and managed to survive. Tests conducted to discover what went wrong showed that the patient had a closed-loop obstruction in her bowel caused by gas. This condition was later found in other babies treated by Letby.

Letby's second victim was Child C, who was born seven weeks premature, weighing a paltry 1 lb, 12 oz (800 g). Despite this fact, he was reportedly in good condition, so the doctors and nurses on duty were caught off-guard when the alarms began to blare, indicating the patient was crashing. Upon entering the room, they discovered Letby was already present and standing over Child C's monitor, even though she wasn't assigned to the patient. She killed Child C on 14 June 2015 by injecting air into his stomach.

Her third victim, Child D, was subjected to having air injected into her bloodstream via her IV. She didn't die immediately, but collapsed three times in the early morning of 22 June 2015. The third time she collapsed resulted in her death, as the doctors were unable to resuscitate her again. Following Child D's demise, the attending healthcare workers observed that the child's skin was noticeably discolored. This is often a symptom of a blood clot, but at the time, the doctors didn't connect it to the pulmonary embolism that killed Child D.

Child E, the fourth victim in Letby's killing spree, was born seven weeks premature with his twin brother, Child F. At the time of his birth, Child E weighed only 3 lbs (1.4 kg). Letby resorted once more to injecting air into her victim's IV, but the twins' mother interrupted her attempt. The mother had gone to retrieve milk for her babies, and when she returned to the room, Letby was interfering with the IV tubes. However, the mother was unaware that Letby was doing anything wrong, simply assuming she was administering drugs for routine treatment. On 4 August 2015, Child E suffered a fatal case of bleeding, which was later determined to be the result of Letby disrupting the patient's nasogastric tube.

On 5 August, only one day after his twin brother's death, Child F narrowly avoided becoming Letby's fifth victim. She laced his feeding bag with a deadly dose of insulin, nearly causing him to succumb to insulin poisoning. A blood sample taken from Child F showed that his insulin levels were "extremely high," while his C-peptide levels were dangerously low. This was a clear indication that he'd been given unauthorized doses of insulin, but the hospital failed to connect it to Letby at the time.

Letby attempted to murder Child G three times over the course of three weeks, with her first attempt occurring on 7 September 2015. Child G was born fifteen weeks premature and weighed merely 1 lb (450 g). Letby first tried to kill the patient when she was 100 days old. This time, Letby administered extra milk and introduced air into the child's nasogastric tube. Child G was transferred to Arrowe Park Hospital for treatment after the incident. When Child G was moved back to the Countess of Chester Hospital, Letby made her second attempt to murder the patient five days later, on 21 September 2015. She tried to murder Child G by poisoning her during the baby's feeding time. The third and final attempt came on 25 September 2015, again by interfering with the patient's nasogastric tube. Although she failed to kill Child G, the young girl is now severely disabled as a direct consequence of Letby's actions.

On 23 October 2015, Letby murdered Child I by inserting air directly into the baby's stomach. This was the fourth attempt by Letby to kill Child I, and her actions were later described as "persistent, calculated, and cold-blooded." In a display of pure audacity, Letby sent a sympathy card to the parents of Child I on the same day that the baby girl's funeral was held. The unmitigated gall to murder a baby and then practically taunt the victim's family through false sympathy showed that Letby possessed a sociopathic personality. Following the death of Child I, she refrained from killing again for about six months.

Letby attempted to murder another pair of twin baby boys, Child L and Child M, on 9 April 2016. She injected insulin into Child L's dextrose bag, and later tests concluded that the baby's insulin levels were "at the very top of the scale that the equipment was capable of measuring." He also had extremely low C-peptide levels from the insulin poisoning. Letby injected air into Child M's IV, which caused him to collapse unexpectedly. His breathing and heart rate dropped to dangerously low levels, and he came incredibly close to dying. Unfortunately, Child M suffered permanent brain damage as a result of the pulmonary embolism he experienced.

There was yet another attempted murder by Letby on 3 June 2015. This occurred only a few days after the potential victim, Child N, was born. He was a hemophiliac, making him susceptible to severe bleeding. Letby took advantage of his condition, using it to cover her attack on him. She forced his nasogastric tube farther down his throat, causing an air embolism and dangerous trauma to Child N. Luckily, the doctors were able to staunch the bleeding and save the patient's life.

Following a vacation to Ibiza, Letby returned to the hospital, itching to kill again. She got her chance when she was assigned to a set of triplets, which included Child O, Child P, and Child Q. At the time of Letby's return, Child O was in perfect health and prepared to go home with his parents. However, he unexpectedly collapsed and died on 23 June 2016. Letby murdered him by injecting air into his nasogastric tube, and also used "significant force" to damage his liver. This introduced an excessive amount of gas into the victim's body, causing him to die. X-rays taken after Child O's death confirmed that he'd been murdered.

On 24 June 2015, only one day after murdering his brother, Letby killed Child P. She utilized the same method as Child O, pumping air into the victim's stomach through his nasogastric tube. She did this while she was feeding him milk. The doctors tried to save Child P's life by transferring him to a hospital better equipped to deal with such a dire case, but he succumbed before he even left the neonatal unit. Almost immediately after the death of Child P, Letby tried to kill Child Q, but failed to end the life of the final triplet. By this point, too many people suspected her of being a murderer, and her entire world was about to unravel.

Investigation and Capture

Back on 2 July 2015, in the midst of Letby's murder spree, the head consultant for the neonatal unit, Dr Stephen Brearey, conducted a review of the three deaths that occurred between 8 June and 22 June 2015. He informed the director of nursing and deputy chief executive, Alison Kelly, that the only nurse on-duty during the unfortunate deaths of Child A, C, and D was Letby. However, Kelly brushed him off and kept Letby active within the neonatal unit. Had she acted on Dr Brearey's information, she would have saved the lives of the subsequent victims.

Dr Brearey continued to follow the alarming trend of infant deaths at the hospital. On 23 October 2015, he looked over the report concerning the death of Child I and found that Letby was on-duty at the time. He was also concerned about the similarities between the deaths of Child C and I. Dr Brearey spoke to his fellow consultant, Dr Ravi Jayaram, informing him of the unusual deaths. The pair contacted the hospital administration about Letby, but they were told not to "make a fuss." Letby remained firmly in the same position at the neonatal unit.

When the hospital administrators sided with Letby over the doctors, forcing them to apologize for "spreading vicious rumors" about her, they had to stop their efforts to prove how dangerous she was to their patients. However, that didn't mean Dr Brearey was ready to just give up. On 8 February 2016, he ordered a review of the various unusual deaths in the neonatal unit. The review found a disturbing number of similarities between 9 patients since June 2015, the same month that Dr Brearey first noticed the suspicious infant mortality rate at the Countess of Chester Hospital.

Following the results of the review, an investigation into the staffing records showed that Letby was on-duty when all 9 babies died. While she wasn't assigned to every patient, she was still present in the neonatal unit at the time. There was a meeting called where the review was discussed, and Letby's possible connection was a talking point. They drew up a report and forwarded it to Ian Harvey, the hospital's medical director. Dr Brearey requested an urgent meeting take place with the executives of the administration, but they continued to drag their feet, and the meeting was delayed until May 2016.

Letby's supporters in the administration attempted to appease the growing discontent among the doctors by moving her to the day shift in April 2016, about a month prior to when the meeting was set to take place. Instead of assuaging their fears, it only increased the amount of suspicion focused on Letby. The rate of infant deaths during the night shift suddenly dropped, while those during the day shift became much higher. Despite this glaringly obvious evidence that she was responsible, the administration was still doing everything in their power to protect her.

On 11 May 2016, the meeting between Dr Brearey, Alison Kelly, and Ian Harvey finally occurred. Dr Brearey laid out his concerns about Letby in an "assurance" document, and included reasons why he believed she was responsible for the spike in unusual deaths in the neonatal unit since June 2015. Kelly and Harvey suggested that other NHS services were to blame for the deaths. They went on to claim that there was "no evidence whatsoever" against Letby, and that her presence at the time of each death was nothing other than "coincidence." At this point, Dr Brearey was certain that the administration was going to dismiss his concerns yet again.

The "tipping point" finally came on 24 June 2016, after the deaths of Child O and P. Dr Brearey called Karen Rees, the duty executive at the hospital, and demanded that she remove Letby from the neonatal unit. Rees, like the others, refused to listen. She insisted that Letby was safe to work there, and that if anything should happen to the other babies being treated, she would be more than happy to take responsibility for it. The doctors chose to take action regardless of the administration's standpoint. They sent Child Q with the team that had arrived to take Child P to another hospital before his untimely death. This ended up saving Child Q's life, as getting him far away from Letby prevented her from murdering him as she'd planned.

With the increased pressure to do something about Letby, the administration finally relented in a small way. They didn't fire her, but they did decide to move her to a clerical position where she no longer had access to the patients. When this caused the unusual deaths to cease, it seemed like a certainty that she was responsible. However, it took another two years before the police were contacted. With the mountain of evidence against her, it didn't take long for the police to connect the dots. This was mostly thanks to the hard work Dr Brearey had done compiling the long list of records concerning Letby and the various unusual deaths surrounding her.

On 3 July 2018, the authorities arrested Letby on suspicion of 8 counts of murder and 6 counts of attempted murder. Her home was then searched, and every death that occurred while she was on-duty at the other hospitals where she'd worked was thoroughly investigated. Letby was bailed out on 6 July 2018, but the police continued their investigation, combing through her entire professional career. They rearrested her on 10 June 2019, this time on suspicion of 8 counts of murder and 9 counts of attempted murder. She was bailed out a second time on 13 June 2019, but later arrested for a third time on 10 November 2020 for 8 counts of murder and 10 counts of attempted murder.

While the case was still ongoing, the Nursing and Midwifery Council placed Letby on an interim suspension on 13 March 2020, with the final decision on whether to revoke her certification pending until the results of her trial were known. On 18 August 2023, following the conclusion of the trial, the Chief Executive and Registrar of the Nursing and Midwifery Council, Andrea Sutcliffe, told the press that Letby "remains suspended from our register, and we will now move forward with our regulatory action, seeking to strike her off the register."

Throughout the investigation, Letby consistently denied all charges against her and blamed the unusual deaths of the infants on the hospital's poor hygiene standards and understaffing of the neonatal unit. Many of her friends and family were similarly supportive of her, speaking out against the hospital for wrongly scapegoating Letby. John and Susan remained by her side every step of the way during the investigation and trial. They stubbornly refused to believe the accusations against their daughter and constantly told the media that Letby was innocent. Her best friend and former colleague, Janet Cox, was also on hand to support Letby. Janet repeatedly expressed her refusal to accept that her friend had done anything wrong.

Another one of Letby's closest friends, only identified as "Dawn," was quoted as saying, "I grew up with Lucy, and not a single thing that I've ever seen or witnessed of Lucy would let me for a moment believe she is capable of the things she's accused of. It is the most out-of-character accusation that you could ever put against Lucy. Think of your most kind, gentle, soft friend and think that they're being accused of harming babies... Unless Lucy turned around and said, "I'm guilty," I will never believe that she's guilty." Just prior to Letby's sentencing, Dawn was asked if she regretted her words, and she asserted, "I stand by that statement."

Motivation

The motivation behind Letby's crimes is difficult to determine. She had a loving family and a happy childhood, so the lack of any obvious reasons for her to become a serial killer has perplexed experts. Many family members of her victims believed she wanted to "play God," determining which patients lived and which ones died. They accused her of having a "misplaced confidence that she could pretty much do whatever she wanted." To them, Letby got an ego boost at controlling the fates of those placed in her care. She enjoyed being the puppet master with both her victims and the people around her who blindly supported her.

Looking at the typical signs of a sociopath, Letby ticks off enough of them to make it likely that she suffers from the psychological disorder. Her lack of empathy for others is obvious, considering the way she callously murdered innocent babies, and even taunted one of her victims' parents with a sympathy card. She used her intelligence, charm, and charisma to manipulate people and resorted to threats against those who resisted. Letby never learned from her mistakes, and whatever punishments were meted out never seemed to be enough to dissuade her from continuing to commit murder. She habitually lied for her own benefit, especially when it came to refuting any accusations that she was a killer. Many of her murders were impulsive, as she decided on a whim to kill her victims, although she could also be very calculating once she made that choice.

It's unclear whether she abused drugs or alcohol, but there's a good chance she indulged in some type of vice. There's also no way to know for sure if she had trouble with her personal responsibilities, like paying her bills, because it appears that her parents were always giving her money for her car, home, food, and other necessities. The inordinately passionate manner in which Letby's many friends and family stood up for her in the face of overwhelming evidence never seemed to be reciprocated. Others were always going to bat for her, but there aren't any accounts of her doing the same for anyone else. This indicates that, on her end, the relationships were merely a tool she could use for her own benefit. All of these things put together, display a true sociopath in action.

Trial

On 10 October 2022, Letby's trial commenced at Manchester Crown Court, with Sir James William Richard Goss serving as judge. By the time she was officially charged, there were 7 counts of murder and 15 counts of attempted murder. She pleaded not guilty to all charges against her. There was an unprecedented amount of secrecy surrounding the identities of the victims and witnesses who testified against Letby. The way their names were kept from the public was "rarely seen outside proceedings involving matters of national security."

The prosecution called Letby a "constant malevolent presence" in the neonatal unit at the Countess of Chester Hospital. Numerous witnesses recalled entering a patient's room to find Letby already there, unaware that they had seen her in the process of committing murder. Other witnesses spoke about catching Letby behaving suspiciously, such as pretending to look busy while a baby was literally bleeding from the mouth. When the police raided her home, they discovered that she'd taken a picture of the sympathy card she sent to the parents of Child I, saving it in her phone like a trophy to commemorate the murder.

There was plenty of evidence to show a horrifying lack of empathy or remorse concerning the infants that died while she was meant to be caring for them. Only two hours after the death of Child M, she bragged in a text message to a friend about winning £135 on a horse race, and later mentioned in a group chat that she wanted to party and drink vodka. When she returned to Chester after her trip to Ibiza, she messaged a friend to say, "Probably be back in with a bang." The very next day, she murdered Child O, followed by Child P, and attempted to kill Child Q.

Further evidence of Letby's inhuman nature came from how she relived her murders. An inspection of her Facebook history showed she had searched for the parents of her victims, and she even did this on the anniversary of Child O's death. Her colleagues revealed that she had to be warned off entering a room where the parents of her victims were grieving on multiple occasions, as she was keen to personally witness the effect her actions had on their families. While she had many people convinced that she was a warm, caring individual, her facade hid the horrible truth: she was a heartless serial killer.

Letby's defense team did their best to portray their client as an innocent woman who was being railroaded and blamed for the mistakes of others. They claimed that she was "a dedicated nurse in a system which has failed," and insisted that there had been a "massive failure of care in a busy hospital neonatal unit—far too great to blame on one person." They further argued that the entire case against their client was "driven by the assumption that someone was doing deliberate harm combined with the coincidence on certain occasions of Miss Letby's presence."

In the case of Child O, who died in part from "extraordinary bleeding" caused by Letby forcing a nasogastric tube down the baby's throat and into his stomach, the defense team proposed that the victim was instead injured by "a rigid wire or tube." They also insisted that the attempted murders of Child F and L were actually Letby using insulin in a therapeutic manner. However, her colleagues testified that there were no therapeutic benefits to using insulin on the patients, and since insulin hadn't been prescribed in either case, it shouldn't have been administered at all. The drug was kept in a locked fridge near the nurses' station, to which Letby had easy access.

A significant piece of evidence included in the trial was the testimony of a consultant doctor who described an incident that occurred in February 2016. He had entered a patient's room and saw Letby hovering over a baby. She was just watching the child passively, despite the fact that the baby appeared to have stopped breathing. Letby's inaction as the patient was rapidly declining alarmed the doctor, and he demanded to know what was going on and why she wasn't doing anything to help the dying child. She responded that the baby had only started to crash moments before he walked in. Fortunately, the patient survived, but the doctor wasn't convinced by her excuse.

Not long after this incident, all seven consultant doctors were in agreement that there was something rotten about the neonatal unit, and word quickly spread that Letby was at the center of the problems. However, every time they brought the matter to the attention of the hospital administration, they brushed it off or threatened the doctors to stop "spreading rumors" and causing a stir over nothing. It baffled them that the administrators were more worried about protecting Letby's reputation than the lives of the babies in their care.

During the period when Letby committed the murders, she stole patient records that belonged to her victims and wrote hundreds of notes with a variety of conflicting messages. One note that was presented in court read, "I am evil, I did this," "I killed them on purpose," and "I couldn't take care of them." Later in the note, she said, "I'll never marry or have children, I'll never know what it's like to have a family." Notes written following her removal from the neonatal unit questioned the police investigation, asking, "Why/how has this happened – what process has led to this current situation? What allegations have been made and by who? Do they have written evidence to support their comments?"

Another note asserted, "I haven't done anything wrong, and they have no evidence, so why have I had to hide away?" Mr Justice Gross commented on the notes, stating that they were "morbid records of the dreadful events" concerning the suffering of her victims and the crimes she committed against them.

Letby denied that she kept the notes to revel in the murders, claiming that she simply had no way of destroying them. This was contradicted by the paper shredder police found in her home. Her personal diary also contained the initials of each of her victims, and they were all placed on the pages that corresponded to the days that they died. More notes were discovered tucked into the diary, including ones that said, "I'm sorry that you couldn't have a chance at life," "I hate my life," "How can life be this way?," "I don't want to do this anymore," and a note written entirely in big, bold letters that simply read, "HELP." Outside of these notes, there was no indication that she felt a compulsion to kill that she was fighting to quell.

In May 2023, Letby took the stand, where she broke down sobbing and swore she "meant no harm," but the doctors and her fellow nurses made her feel incompetent. Her excuse for the contents of her notes that seemed to confess to murder was that it was misplaced guilt. She told the court, "I felt at the time that if I'd done something wrong I must be such an evil, awful person. I'd somehow been incompetent and had done something wrong which had affected those babies." According to her, many of the notes were written during times of great distress and mental anguish, so their contents shouldn't be taken as representative of reality. During her testimony, she frequently contradicted herself, gave confusing accounts of events, and grew increasingly frustrated with the questions asked by the prosecution.

At one point, Letby spoke about the negative effect the murder allegations had on her mental health. She said, "I don't think you can be accused of anything worse than that. I just changed as a person, my mental health deteriorated, I felt isolated from my friends on the unit. From a self-confidence point of view, it made me question everything about myself." Letby lost her composure several times while in the witness box, and she asked at these times that the court allow her to take an unplanned break. Observers commented that she only became emotional when talking about herself and how the case affected her personally. She never shed a single tear for the enormous loss of brand new life that occurred under her watch.

The trial lasted nine months, and the jury was finally sent to deliberate the verdict on 10 July 2023. The deliberation went on for nearly a month, and the verdicts were returned over ten days. The first verdict was returned on 8 August 2023, while the final verdict came in on 18 August 2023. Ultimately, Letby was found guilty on 7 counts of murder and 7 counts of attempted murder. She was found not guilty on 2 counts of attempted murder, and the jury was unable to reach a verdict on 6 counts of attempted murder.

Letby was sentenced on 21 August 2023 to life imprisonment with 14 whole life orders. This is the harshest sentence available under current British law. She is only the fourth woman in the history of the United Kingdom to receive such a sentence. Mr Justice Goss called Letby's murders "a cruel, calculated and cynical campaign of child murder involving the smallest and most vulnerable of children." At the end of his closing speech, he added that "there was a deep malevolence bordering on sadism," and called her out on having "no remorse." He also declared that "there are no mitigating factors" to consider with her crimes, and "the offenses are of sufficient severity to require a whole life order."

Aftermath

Letby, her parents, and her friends chose not to attend her sentencing hearing, which meant they didn't have to listen to the victim impact statements or the denouncement of her by the court. Because of this, the Secretary of State for Justice, Alex Chalk, said that the government was going to "look at options to change the law at the earliest opportunity" in order to compel future defendants to attend their sentencing hearings. Prime Minister Rishi Sunak also stated that the government planned to introduce legislation to Parliament that would force convicted criminals to attend their sentencing hearings, with a penalty of more time in prison if they refused.

Right after the trial, Letby was taken to HMP Low Newton, a high-security prison in the village of Brasside, not far from the county of Durham. It is currently home to some of Britain's most infamous murderers, such as Joanna Dennehy, Tracey Connelly, and Rose West. Dennehy was the first woman to receive a whole life order after killing 3 victims over a 10-day period in 2013. Letby chafed at being held in prison, hating the confinement and lack of control over her own life. She complained that she couldn't even use the bathroom whenever she wished, and the lack of privacy made it difficult to get settled.

On 15 September 2023, Letby filed an appeal with the Court of Appeal Criminal Division. The court confirmed that she had appealed all of her convictions, but no date for a hearing has been set. The Crown Prosecution Service announced on 25 September 2023 that there would be a retrial for the 6 counts of attempted murder that the jury couldn't come to a decision on. The date for the retrial has been tentatively set as 10 June 2024, but it will not commence until after the Court of Appeal Criminal Division decides if they will grant Letby a hearing for the appeal against her existing convictions.

In the wake of Letby's murders, reforms have begun to hold NHS managers and healthcare administrators accountable for mismanagement of their hospitals and clinics. Investigations into her work at previous facilities have continued, with the authorities sifting through every patient she ever came into contact with, hoping to determine whether or not she had a hand in even more deaths, illnesses, or trauma.

Since Letby's departure from the Countess of Chester Hospital, the neonatal unit has experienced only a single death in seven years. While they are no longer allowed to care for babies in critical condition as a direct result of the administration ignoring Letby's actions for such a long time, they only lost two or three infants per year prior to her arrival. It should have been obvious much earlier that Letby was the reason for the disturbingly high mortality rate, but now it's crystal clear that she was the only person who could have been responsible for the murders of all those innocent babies.

Chapter 10

Charles Cullen

Charles Cullen was a nurse and serial killer from New Jersey whose crimes went on for more than a decade-and-a-half before he was caught. He was convicted for killing 29 victims in both New Jersey and Pennsylvania. His murders occurred at seven different hospitals across those two states, and he unbelievably continued to secure nursing jobs despite being fired for serious infractions in multiple instances. This case was famously depicted in the 2022 Netflix film *The Good Nurse*, which starred British actor Eddie Redmayne as Cullen.

Background and Family

Charles Edward Cullen was born on 22 February 1960 in West Orange, New Jersey, to Edmond and Florence Cullen (née Ward). The family had strong Roman Catholic roots, and that carried over into how the couple raised their eight children. They were a working-class family, so money was always extremely tight. With their kids outnumbering them 4 to 1, Edmond and Florence struggled to maintain order. The older children were often left in charge of their younger siblings, which gave them free rein to torture their little brothers and sisters.

Edmond worked as a bus driver, and on 17 September 1960, less than seven months after Cullen was born, he died in an accident, leaving Florence on her own to manage all eight children, including her very young infant. She was from England, having married Edmond after World War II as a war bride, and left her own family behind. Since they were all still across the Atlantic Ocean, she didn't have much support to fall back on once her husband was gone. This forced her to rely more on her older children, which caused them to resent their younger siblings even more.

Upbringing

According to Cullen, his childhood was miserable. He was raised alongside two brothers and five sisters in a wooden-framed, three-story house on Kling Street, which was located in a low-income section of town. As the youngest of the family's eight children, he would either be neglected or a target for abuse. He never knew his father, and his mother was barely keeping the family together. Whatever meager funds they'd had prior to Edmond's death were long gone by the time Cullen was a few years old. The family had very little money for things like toys or clothes. Cullen couldn't remember owning a single thing that wasn't a hand-me-down from his older siblings. His older brothers rarely missed an opportunity to remind him that all of his possessions really belonged to them.

In addition to being poor, he experienced a significant amount of bullying. His elder siblings tormented him even worse than they did the other younger ones, but he also received plenty of abuse from his classmates and the boys who dated his sisters. Despite being so young, Cullen was already exhibiting signs of severe depression. When he was 9 years old, he attempted suicide by drinking the chemicals that came with a chemistry set his teenage brother had gotten as a recent birthday gift. Instead of showing concern for Cullen, his brother was furious at him for ruining his present, and the rest of his siblings were similarly angry that the family's limited funds were now being siphoned off to pay the hospital bill.

Throughout his childhood, the one bright spot for Cullen was his mother. He adored her, treasuring the time they spent together more than anything else in his life. Unfortunately, she was constantly busy taking care of the family and their home, so the two didn't get a chance to have much one-on-one time. For his eleventh birthday, Florence took him to the Turtle Back Zoo, which first opened in town on 3 June 1963. It was one of the few truly good days he could later recall from his youth, and he kept the small lion figurine she bought for him at the gift shop with him everywhere he lived, up until his arrest.

Schooling

Cullen began his academic career at Our Lady of Lourdes School in West Orange, which he attended from preschool to eighth grade. It was a Catholic school, and because of the family's religious background, Florence wanted her children to have a Catholic-based education. The school was only 3 miles away from his home, and he rode the bus there with a few of his older siblings. However, they would often "ditch" him to sit with their friends, leaving him to sit alone and feel unwanted. He was shy as a child and had some unique quirks that made him an easy target for bullying. It didn't help that his own siblings seemed to spearhead the abuse—when his peers saw the way his brothers and sisters treated him, they viewed it as an open invitation to do the same.

As he got older, the bullying he experienced only got worse. With his siblings having moved on to high school, he was forced to ride the bus alone. Cullen hated taking the bus and begged his mother to drive him, but she was too busy and refused. The other children would stick gum in his hair and hit him with their books or backpacks as they walked by him. They also taunted him for his appearance, as he was very thin and awkward-looking. In a double reference to the ethnic slurs used by American soldiers for the Vietnamese people and the Chinese soldiers supporting North Vietnam during the then-ongoing Vietnam War, they called him "Chinky Charlie."

After finishing his primary education, Cullen attended West Orange High School, a public school, unlike Our Lady of Lourdes. The abuse he received at his new school became more severe. He was being physically attacked almost on a daily basis, and he was both angry and ashamed that he wasn't strong enough to stand up for himself. Cullen looked for ways to toughen up, but nothing seemed to work for him. His daydreams were filled with revenge fantasies, always thinking up horrific plots that would make his tormentors suffer before killing them. At the time, he didn't have the power to make these fantasies become reality, but he never forgot them. These feelings extended to the authority figures in his life who failed to protect him, which he viewed as a silent endorsement of the bullies' actions.

It was Cullen's belief that at least part of the reason he was targeted was due to his intelligence. He was much smarter and more well-read than his peers, which made him stand out. In high school, he read Crime and Punishment by Fyodor Dostoevsky, which had a huge impact on his worldview. In the novel, the main character, Rodion Romanovich Raskolnikov, convinces himself that if he kills an unscrupulous pawn broker, the woman's death will allow him to escape from poverty and go on to do great things. He rationalizes his actions by the mindset that extraordinary people should be permitted to take any action, including murder, if it removes the obstacles standing in their way in order to achieve their goals, which would benefit all of mankind. This idea that cold-blooded murder could be justified festered in his mind, eventually becoming a part of his psyche.

When Cullen was in the middle of his senior year, he suffered a serious blow that changed the course of his life. On 6 December 1977, Florence was in a car accident while Cullen's older sister Alice was driving, sustaining grievous injuries that required her to be rushed to the hospital, where she later died. Cullen was furious at the hospital staff and his family because they didn't bother to contact him until after she was dead. He was devastated when he heard the news, and the loss of his mother was compounded by the fact that the hospital decided to cremate her body before informing Cullen of Florence's death. Realistically, the family was too poor to bear the costs of holding a funeral, and his elder siblings authorized the cremation, but Cullen had wanted his mother's body returned to him anyway. He blamed his sister, his family, and the hospital staff for taking Florence away from him. It was a transgression he would never forget.

Military Service

After graduating high school, Cullen felt adrift without Florence to serve as his anchor. Unsure about what he wanted to do with his life and having nothing left to keep him at home, he decided to enlist in the United States Navy in 1978. He completed basic training, and the psychological exams administered to all incoming naval personnel showed that he was capable of enduring long periods of time isolated and in cramped spaces, making him a good candidate to work on a submarine. Cullen had essentially been training for this his whole life, since he lived in a small house with too many people and had a very limited social life.

Based on his psychological profile, Cullen was assigned to serve aboard the USS Woodrow Wilson, a *Lafayette*-class ballistic missile submarine. During his service, he was promoted to the rank of petty officer second class, and was tasked with operating the Poseidon missiles carried by the vessel. However, he still never really fit in with his fellow sailors, and suffered from bullying and hazing enacted by the other crewmen. His occasional bizarre behavior did nothing to quell this treatment.

About a year after joining the crew, his leading petty officer stumbled upon him wearing scrubs, a surgical mask, and latex gloves stolen from the infirmary instead of his requisite uniform while seated at the controls for the submarine's missile systems. He received disciplinary action over the incident, yet he refused to explain why he chose to dress like that. When word of the incident got out to the rest of the sailors aboard the *Woodrow Wilson*, the bullying intensified. At that point, his commanding officer contacted the U.S. Navy's headquarters in Washington and recommended that he be reassigned.

In 1980, Cullen was transferred to a position on the *USS Canopus*, s *Simon Lake*-class submarine tender. Their job was to refit, repair, and resupply the submarines carrying Polaris missiles and the nuclear-armed ballistic missiles themselves. It was an assignment with less pressure, which the Navy hoped would alleviate some of the behavioral issues he'd displayed aboard the *Woodrow Wilson*. It seemed like the best decision for his mental health, but he only got worse once he was on the *Canopus*. He attempted suicide five times, forcing his commanding officer to have him committed to the Navy psychiatric ward on multiple occasions over the next four years. In 1984, they ended up granting him a medical discharge for undisclosed reasons.

Nursing School

After being discharged from the Navy, Cullen enrolled in the nursing school run by Mountainside

Hospital in Montclair, New Jersey. In a complete reversal of his experience during his primary and secondary school years, he excelled there, as intelligence was viewed as a good thing when seeking to become a caregiver. He even became popular enough with his fellow nursing students to be elected the class president. It's uncertain what brought on the change in his behavior and attitude, but it's likely that his military service taught him the self-discipline required to hide his true personality and project one more acceptable by societal standards. He graduated from the program in 1986, and was immediately able to find a good job.

Professional Career

The first place where Cullen worked after nursing school was St. Barnabas Medical Center in Livingston, New Jersey. He came onboard in June 1987 and served in their burn unit, which is still the only state-certified burn treatment facility in New Jersey, as well as one of the largest in the entire country. He worked with patients of all ages and severity of injuries. Considering the burn unit treated an average of 350 burn victims each year, Cullen had plenty of opportunities to begin committing murder.

While in nursing school, Cullen met a woman who worked as a computer programmer named Adrienne Taub, and they started dating. They got married on 7 June 1987, right around the time when he got the job at St. Barnabas. That same year, his older brother James died of a drug overdose at the age of 31. Due to his feelings concerning his family and the way they'd treated him, he chose not to attend the funeral service. In October 1988,

Casey, the first of the couple's two daughters, was born. Their second daughter, Jillian, arrived in December 1991.

Cullen suffered a professional setback when he was fired from his job at St. Barnabas in January 1992, after the hospital administration suspected him of tampering with the IV bags given to patients. However, they failed to report their suspicions to anyone, and kept the circumstances surrounding his termination quiet. This allowed Cullen to get a job at a new hospital, and one month later, he was hired at St. Luke's Warren Hospital in Phillipsburg, New Jersey. While there were a few complaints from patients about his conduct, the administration dismissed them as "unfounded." He had managed to put on the facade of a normal, happy family man for nearly half a decade, but it was while working at Warren that his mask began to slip.

Cullen started showing disturbing behavior at home, and Adrienne became increasingly worried about the safety of their daughters. He once burned a book that Casey was reading because he didn't like the way the cover looked. When he was forced to be around people he didn't like or annoyed him, he liked to spike their drinks with lighter fluid as a means of revenge. On one occasion, while Adrienne was out of town for an extended period of time, he left their daughters with a babysitter for a week and refused to divulge where he went or what he was doing for the duration of his absence. Cullen also had a tendency to act in a manner that was off-putting, like asking invasive questions or staring over long at others without speaking in social situations.

He allegedly took their two dogs down into the basement of their home in Phillipsburg and beat them to the point that Adrienne could hear their cries from the bedroom. When she confronted her husband, he told her that he was simply "training them." In another incident, Cullen stuffed their Yorkshire terrier into a bowling bag as "punishment" when it peed on the living room carpet. Animal abuse is one of the characteristics of a serial killer's psychological profile, and the way he treated their pets definitely qualified as abusive behavior.

A former neighbor who lived near Cullen's Phillipsburg home alleged that he frequently left the dogs outside for hours, tying them up and refusing to bring them inside during extreme weather conditions. It got bad enough that multiple people reported him to the Society for the Prevention of Cruelty to Animals, who investigated the situation and ended up rescuing the abused animals. As his violent tendencies got worse, Adrienne feared that he would soon shift his focus from abusing their pets to hurting her and their children.

As the inevitable dissolution of their marriage was imminent, Cullen started to drink heavily and stopped taking his depression medication. According to Adrienne, her husband slept on the couch in their living room for about three years preceding their divorce, having started doing so not long after Jillian was conceived. He became reclusive, refused to take her out, and barely had any interaction with her. During this time, he would drink and drive frequently, but was only stopped and issued a DUI once. In 1993, Adrienne finally filed for divorce, citing his "extreme cruelty" and "unusual behavior" as the reason for seeking to end their marriage, and she attempted to gain full custody of Casey and Jillian.

Unfortunately, the court deemed that Cullen would never harm their children, and an order of joint custody was finalized. Adrienne moved to Roselle Park, NJ, and Cullen rented an apartment across town from where they used to live in Phillipsburg. Their daughters were still very young, but they could still sense the tense atmosphere in the home around the time their parents' marriage ended. Owing to the way he'd treated them in the years leading up to the divorce, Casey and Jillian found being alone with him unpleasant, and as they got older, they resented having to spend time with their father, as it meant their schooling and social lives were interrupted whenever Cullen had custody of them.

Between the divorce proceedings, his fragile state of mind, and dealing with two angry daughters who hated having to see him, Cullen began to lash out at his ex-wife. Adrienne filed a domestic violence complaint against him in January 1993. In the complaint, she noted that his access to many different types of drugs as a hospital nurse put her and their daughters in danger. After filing a second complaint later that year, she also requested a restraining order, hoping this would alter their custody agreement. The restraining order was granted in light of the fact that after each complaint was filed, Cullen attempted suicide. It seemed like he was using suicide attempts as a method of controlling and manipulating the people in his life. While the court temporarily granted Adrienne full custody, and Cullen's visits had to be supervised, it eventually reverted back to the original agreement after a year.

In the wake of his divorce, Cullen claimed he wanted to quit nursing altogether, but the amount of money he had to pay Adrienne for child support and alimony prevented him from switching job fields. His behavior became more erratic after the upheaval of the divorce. In March 1993, he went on a dinner date with a fellow nurse named Michelle Tomlinson. She turned him down the next time he asked her out, but he had already developed an infatuation with her. Following her rejection, his obsession with her grew. He called her incessantly, even though Michelle had begged him to stop. While at work, he followed her around the hospital, and at one point, attempted to propose, having already purchased an engagement ring for her. When she turned him down, his obsessive behavior escalated.

On 23 March 1993, he drove to her home in the middle of the night and broke in. Michelle was fast asleep at the time—as was her very young son. They were fortunate that he decided to leave without harming them, as many others weren't so lucky. When Michelle found out what he'd done, she reported Cullen to the police, and he was arrested. While in custody, he confessed to a police officer that he'd created a fantasy where Michelle was his girlfriend, and his mental health issues caused him to believe it was true. He pleaded guilty to misdemeanor trespassing, receiving a sentence of one-year probation. Following his arrest, Cullen attempted suicide yet again.

The hospital administrators urged Cullen to take a break from work and seek help. He took a two-month leave of absence and received treatment for severe depression from two different psychiatric facilities. Before the year was out, he made two more suicide attempts. Throughout his struggles with his mental health, he continued to work at Warren, and the other staff members were mostly supportive of him, doing their best to uplift their fellow caregiver in his time of need. Little did they know that he was heartlessly murdering patients during their time of need behind the staff's back.

At the beginning of September 1993, the son of an elderly cancer patient told the hospital staff that Cullen had entered his mother's room and used a needle to inject her with an unknown substance. He wasn't assigned to the woman, and when she died the following day, her son insisted that she was murdered. The administration put Cullen and the other nurses on-duty when the patient died through a lie detector test. He passed and remained employed at Warren until December 1993.

Several months after leaving his previous job, Cullen was hired at Hunterdon Medical Center in Flemington, New Jersey, in April 1994. He worked in their intensive care unit for three years and departed in October 1996, moving to Morristown Memorial Hospital in November 1996. Due to his substandard performance, he was fired in August 1997, leaving him unemployed for the next six months. Cullen searched the area for a new job, but word had started to spread about him, and he had a poor reputation in New Jersey. This led to him looking for work across the state border.

Cullen managed to land a position at the Liberty Nursing and Rehabilitation Center in Allentown,

Pennsylvania. He was assigned to a ward in the facility where all the patients were dependent on respirators. His stint there didn't last long, and he was fired in October 1998. The reason for his dismissal included accusations that he was dispensing drugs to patients at unscheduled times, and he was also caught going into a patient's room with multiple syringes. Cullen attempted to forcibly inject an unprescribed drug into him, but the patient struggled to stop him. Their scuffle resulted in Cullen breaking the patient's arm. Unbeknownst to the facility managers, he was responsible for the death of another patient. They instead blamed one of his fellow nurses for the fatal mistake.

Somehow, Cullen was able to continuously find work, regardless of the fact that even before factoring in the murders, his caregiving abilities had deteriorated significantly. He was also mentally unstable and had a concerning work history. However, this was before there were proper systems in place to document, report, and share information on nurses with employment problems and mental health issues. In addition, there was a national shortage of nurses at that time, and medical facilities were desperate to find anyone with the proper qualifications willing to work under less-than-desirable conditions. Cullen was only unemployed for roughly a month, and in November 1998, he was hired by Easton Hospital, located in Easton, Pennsylvania. Again, he didn't remain there for very long, leaving in March 1999 to avoid questions about the unusual death of a patient.

Later, in March 1999, Cullen was hired at Lehigh Valley Hospital-Cedar Crest in Allentown. On 11 January

2000, he lit a charcoal grill in his bathtub, hoping to be poisoned by the carbon monoxide. When his neighbors smelled the heavy smoke, they contacted emergency services, and both the police and fire department were dispatched to the scene. Cullen was confined to a psychiatric facility and put under observation, but they released him the next day. He spent around a year and a half at Lehigh Valley, voluntarily resigning in April 2000. His next job was in June 2000 at St. Luke's Hospital in Bethlehem, Pennsylvania.

Cullen's tenure at St. Luke's was rocky from the start, but fate seemed to be working against his future victims. According to Pat Medellin, a critical care nurse at the hospital, St. Luke's was in the process of getting a loan for the construction of a new site to house their campus. Any negative publicity would've tarnished their reputation and prevented the project from proceeding, so keeping the incidents with Cullen quiet helped them avoid losing out on a major deal. That's why when a fellow nurse discovered he was stealing medications from the hospital, the administration offered him a deal to resign and be given a neutral recommendation instead of being fired. He accepted the deal and resigned but was escorted by security guards from the building. His departure from St. Luke's occurred in June 2002, two years after he began working there.

Within a month, Cullen got a job at Sacred Heart Hospital in Allentown, starting on 8 July 2002. However, his poor reputation in the city was well-known by that point, and the entire nursing staff threatened to quit in protest if he wasn't fired. On 24 July 2002, Sacred Heart terminated his employment. He returned to his home state after getting fired and found a new job at Somerset Medical Center in Somerset, New Jersey, in September 2002. It was at Somerset where his hidden murder spree would finally be uncovered. When the hospital administration became aware of the truth about his employment history, including the fact that he had lied on his job application, they fired him in October 2003.

Murders

Cullen started his career as a serial killer while working at St. Barnabas. His first victim was 72-year-old John W. Yengo, a municipal judge from Jersey City, who died on 11 June 1988. He murdered John by administering a lethal amount of IV drugs, causing the patient to overdose. His second confirmed victim was Lucy Vigilone Mugavero, a 90-year-old Phillipsburg native who died on 9 March 1993 at St. Luke's Warren Hospital. She was once a garment worker and later became the mayor of Phillipsburg and chairman of the Delaware River Joint Toll Bridge Commission.

After being cleared by the hospital administration, Cullen went on to kill Mary Natoli, a former silk mill employee and grandmother from Phillipsburg who was 85 years old when she died on 23 July 1993. A little over a month later, on 1 September 1993, he murdered Helen Dean, a 91-year-old from Lopatcong Township, New Jersey. She was in the hospital battling breast cancer, and it was in her room where Cullen was found by her son when he wasn't assigned to her. He had injected an overdose of digoxin, a heart medication, causing her to die the following day. Despite this, he managed to pass the lie detector test and avoid suspicion. Helen's son, Larry, swore he would find the person responsible for his mother's death, but he too, died of cancer, succumbing to the disease in 2001.

While working at Hunterdon, Cullen murdered 71-year-old LeRoy Sinn on 21 January 1996. He was a patent attorney and part of the Gardeners of Somerset Valley club. On 31 May 1996, Cullen killed Earl Young, a 76-year-old stock clerk at Flemington Cut Glass. His next victim was 49-year-old Catherine Dext, who died on 9 June 1996. She worked at the Edna Mahan Correctional Facility for Women in Union Township. A few weeks later, Cullen murdered Frank Mazzacco on 24 June 1996, a 66-year-old who worked in the Trenton public school system for 34 years and served several terms as the president of the teachers' union. Cullen's final victim at Hunterdon was Jesse Eichlin, who he killed on 10 July 1996. Jesse was 81 years old when he died, and was a former carpenter and farmer who helped build an addition to a church in Franklin Township, New Jersey.

Cullen murdered Ottomar Schramm, a 78-year-old who was the son of two missionaries proselytizing in Nicaragua when he was born. At the time of his murder on 30 December 1998, he was a native of Bethlehem, Pennsylvania, and had a wife and three children who survived him. He was the only known victim from Cullen's time at Easton. Similarly, the only person he killed while at Lehigh Valley was Matthew Mattern, a 22-year-old from Shamokin, Pennsylvania, who died on 31 August 1999. Matthew was Cullen's youngest victim and was in the hospital following a car accident in which he received severe burns all over his body.

On 22 June 2001, while working at St. Luke's, Cullen murdered Irene Krapf, a 79-year-old from Tamaqua, Pennsylvania. She had 8 children and 22 grandchildren and ran a taxi company out of the family home with her husband. A 72-year-old named William Park became another of Cullen's victims on 8 November 2001. He was an upholsterer and veteran of the Korean War who resided in Franklin Township, Pennsylvania. Samuel Spangler, an 80-year-old from Bethlehem, was murdered on 9 January 2002. He was a machine operator at Stroh Brewing Company before retiring and enjoying the company of his large family. The next victim, also from Bethlehem, was 82-year-old Daniel George, who died on 5 May 2002. He owned George's Foodliner in his hometown and Danny's Restaurant and Lounge in Hanover Township, Pennsylvania.

On 2 June 2002, Edward O'Toole, a retired World War II Navy veteran and district sales manager for A.O. Smith Water Heater Company, was murdered by Cullen. He was 76 years old at the time of his death. With the bodies rapidly piling up, some of the staff at St. Luke's became suspicious of their co-worker. Seven of them contacted the Lehigh County district attorney and told them of their belief that he'd killed some of his patients with drugs. The authorities never bothered to look into Cullen's past employment history or criminal records, and the case was dropped within nine months due to a lack of evidence.

After moving to Somerset Medical Center, Cullen murdered Eleanor Stoecker, a 60-year-old Bedminster, New Jersey native, on 12 February 2003. She was a retired medical assistant, as well as the mother of tri-state area radio personality Zack Martin. On 23 February 2003, a day after Cullen's 43rd birthday, he killed 74-year-old Joyce E. Mangini. She was a homemaker from Raritan, New Jersey, who was a passionate cook and crocheter. 89-year-old Giacomino "Jack" Toto died later that same day. He was a mechanic for 25 years and had his own vegetable stand.

John J. Shanagher, an 83-year-old from Bridgewater, New Jersey, became another of Cullen's victims on 11 March 2003. He had fought in World War II, serving in one of the army companies that took part in the liberation of European concentration camps. A Middlesex, New Jersey native and homemaker named Dorthea K. Hoagland was killed on 6 April 2003 at the age of 80. Melvin T. Simcoe, a 66-year-old Korean War veteran and the district manager for Bellcore of Livingston, was murdered on 5 May 2003. Ten days later, Cullen murdered Michael T. Strenko of Manville, New Jersey. Michael had been a star athlete in high school and was working for Fisher Scientific when he died.

The reign of terror carried out by Cullen continued with the death of Florian J. Gall on 28 June 2003. He was a 68-year-old from Whitehouse Station, New Jersey, and was a pastor of Our Lady of Lourdes Roman Catholic Church and Hunterdon County vicar for the Diocese of Metuchen. Pasquale M. Napolitano, an 80-year-old World War II veteran and the security manager for two Village

Supermarkets locations, was killed on 13 July 2003. Cullen's subsequent victim, Christopher B. Hardgrove, was a local 38-year-old who died on 11 August 2003. Christopher was a carpenter and left behind two daughters. 70-year-old Krishnakant Upadhya was murdered on 20 September 2003, followed soon after by 83-year-old James R. Strickland on 23 September 2003. James was still grieving the loss of his wife when Cullen ended his life, and he was buried with the harmonica he loved to play. The final victim was Edward P. Zizik, a 73-year-old from Three Bridges, New Jersey, who died on 21 October 2003 from low blood sugar after being given an excessive amount of digoxin. He spent 30 years working as an electrical engineer and was a volunteer at the very hospital where he was killed.

Investigation and Capture

Pat Medellin was among the first to attempt to get law enforcement involved when she suspected Cullen of harming patients. She was a critical care nurse at St. Luke's during the same period when he worked there, and she thought it was strange that while Cullen had resigned from his position, he was escorted from the building by security. Having witnessed this personally, it made her think back on previous incidents involving Cullen that she dismissed at the time, just like everybody else.

There were two patients in stable condition assigned to Cullen, who both died within the span of a week. Pat went over the records for 67 deaths at the hospital, which was when she discovered a major discrepancy: he was noted as being on duty during 40 of those 67 deaths, despite the fact that he should have only been working when about 20 of them occurred. It appeared that he was treating many patients to which he wasn't assigned and even operated in an official capacity when he was off-duty. Pat alerted her manager to this fact, but the hospital administrators denied her assessment was correct. She then went to the Pennsylvania State Police, but they were slow to investigate and closed the case without finding any evidence to implicate Cullen in the deaths.

During Cullen's time at St. Luke's, when Helen Dean's son Larry accused a nurse of injecting something with a syringe into his mother just before her death, Cullen was cleared during the subsequent internal investigation, which allowed him to keep murdering his patients. It wasn't until after Edward Zizik's death when a Somerset nurse and former friend of Cullen named Amy Loughren informed the New Jersey State Police that Cullen was responsible for the death of a patient, that an official investigation managed to turn up enough evidence against him for an arrest. He was fired from Somerset on 31 October 2003 for lying on his job application.

After Amy learned more about Cullen's history concerning his employment issues, stealing drugs, and links to the deaths of many patients, she agreed to aid the police in getting more evidence against her fellow nurse and former friend. They tasked her with going over to his home after she got off work to have conversations with him while wearing a wire to record what he said. The evidence gathered from her undercover efforts eventually gave the authorities enough probable cause to make an arrest. On 12 December 2003, the police arrested Cullen while he was dining with friends at a local restaurant.

Motivation

While Cullen insisted that he only killed patients to end their suffering, the truth is rooted in his background. Many of his victims were people who were once in positions of authority or contained ties to institutions that Cullen felt had wronged him. He killed lawyers, judges, mayors, schoolteachers, and members of the Catholic Church. They were all the exact kinds of people that turned a blind eye to the torment he endured throughout his childhood, sometimes even contributing to the abuse themselves. It didn't matter that his victims had never met him until they came to his hospital—they represented the people that Cullen hated, and he intended to get his long-awaited, misguided revenge at any cost.

Trial

When Cullen was initially arrested, he was only charged with 1 count of murder and 1 count of attempted murder. After confessing to detectives that he'd killed at least 40 victims during his 16-year career as a nurse, the charges were adjusted accordingly. In April 2004, Cullen accepted a plea deal where he would plead guilty to 13 counts of murder and 2 counts of attempted murder, as well as cooperate with authorities in their still-ongoing investigation in exchange for removing the death penalty from his sentence. In May 2004, he pleaded guilty to 3 additional murder charges in New Jersey, and in

November 2004, he pleaded guilty to 6 counts of murder and 3 counts of attempted murder in Pennsylvania.

On 2 March 2006, Cullen was sentenced to 11 consecutive life sentences without parole. He was taken to the New Jersey State Prison in Trenton to serve out his sentences, but was brought to Allentown on 10 March 2006 to face his sentencing for the murders in Pennsylvania. At this point, since Cullen already knew he was never getting out of prison, he chose to taunt the judge for nearly 30 minutes straight, until he was finally gagged by stuffing cloth in his mouth and securing it with duct tape. In the end, he was given 6 more life sentences.

Aftermath

Because Cullen's crimes escaped notice for so long due to the lack of any mechanism to report suspicious activity or easily access previous employment records, New Jersey, Pennsylvania, and 35 other states enacted new laws to fix that problem. They wanted to make it a requirement to disclose any worrisome activity of healthcare workers, while removing the fears of liability that dissuaded many administrators from making official reports. In New Jersey, the 2004 Patient Safety Act increased the responsibility put on hospitals to report "serious preventable adverse events," while the supplemental 2005 Enhancement Act compelled hospitals to report certain details about employees to the New Jersey Division of Consumer Affairs, as well as mandating that complaints and disciplinary records relating to patient care be kept for at least seven years. The New Jersey laws served as a model for nearly every other state's subsequent adoption of similar legislation.

Conclusion

Understanding what drives a person to become a murderer, especially someone who chooses to enter a healthcare profession, can help prevent similar crimes. While there's no excuse for killing patients, some of the problems brought up by the killers in this book aren't unlike the complaints of many dedicated healthcare workers. Too many patients and heavy workloads, issues with understaffing, and pressure from the administrations to process more patients in order to make more money can affect good caregivers just as much as the bad ones. While most don't become serial killers, it can still cause a severe strain on their mental health.

The adoption of strict screening, monitoring, and reporting procedures has helped to alleviate some of the problems that allowed certain serial killers to operate within the walls of medical facilities for such a long time, but there are still many problems that have yet to be addressed. Healthcare professionals need better support systems and considerations to reduce the risk of burnout and stress-induced mental health crises. They should be encouraged to have open conversations about the challenges they face without the fear of disciplinary action from their employers, and they should be permitted to report any concerning behavior they witness from their peers without worrying that they'll be seen as discriminatory.

Most of the serial killers covered in this book had complaints made against them well before they were caught, only to be dismissed by hospital administrators and medical facility managers. In some cases, those making the complaints were punished, while the person committing murder escaped the consequences of their actions for a little longer. The fact that the higher-ups prioritized the public reputation of their institutions over the safety of their patients is unacceptable. The culture that created this mindset needs to change before any meaningful reforms can take place. Until making money is no longer the primary goal of the healthcare industry, people will always be less important than profit margins.

It can be very unsettling to think about caregivers transforming into life-takers. Fortunately, it doesn't happen often, which is why cases of serial killers in the medical field attract so much morbid attention from the media. Most healthcare professionals genuinely care about their patients and work hard to save lives. Of course, the small number of doctors and nurses who stray from their professional oaths and commit terrible crimes against those in their care wreak enough havoc to make people think twice about going to a medical facility for help. That's why it's important to stress that the actions of a few bad apples aren't representative of the medical community as a whole.

References

About: Stephan Letter. (n.d.). DBpedia. https://dbpedia.org/page/Stephan_Letter

Beckwith-Wiedemann syndrome. (n.d.). Childrenshospital.org. https://www.childrenshospital.org/conditions/beckwith-wiedemann-syndrome

Black, I. (2001, September 12). Swiss Angel of Death admits 27 killings. *The Guardian.* https://www.theguardian.com/world/2001/sep/12/ianblack

Blanco, J. I. (n.d.-a). *Arnfinn Nessett.* Murderpedia.org. https://murderpedia.org/male.N/n/nesset-arnfinn.htm

Blanco, J. I. (n.d.-b). *Donald Harvey.* Murderpedia.org. https://murderpedia.org/male.H/h/harvey-donald.htm

Blanco, J. I. (n.d.-c). *Orville Majors.* Murderpedia.org. https://murderpedia.org/male.M/m/majors-orville.htm

Blanco, J. I. (n.d.-d). *Roger Andermatt.* Murderpedia.org. https://murderpedia.org/male.A/a/andermatt-roger.htm

Blanco, J. I. (n.d.-e). *Sandy Charles.* Murderpedia.org. https://murderpedia.org/male.C/c/charles-sandy.htm

Blanco, J. I. (n.d.-f). *Stephan Letter.* Murderpedia.org. https://murderpedia.org/male.L/l/letter-stephan.htm

Call, M. (2003, December 18). Those who know Cullen see different sides ** Lawyer, neighbor say he was kind. Ex-wife called him cruel. *Morning Call.* https://www.mcall.com/2003/12/18/those-who-know-cullen-see-different-sides-lawyer-neighbor-say-he-was-kind-ex-wife-called-him-cruel/

Carter, H., & Killelea, A. (2020, February 8). *How a newly-qualified doctor restored faith in Hyde after Dr Death*. Manchester Evening News.
https://www.manchestereveningnews.co.uk/news/uk-news/doctor-hyde-harold-shipman-speaks-17701677

Certificat d'aptitude professionnelle / CAP. (n.d.). Insee.Fr.
https://www.insee.fr/en/metadonnees/definition/c2136

CHAMBET Ludivine. (n.d.). Serial Killer Database Wiki; Fandom, Inc.
https://skdb.fandom.com/wiki/CHAMBET_Ludivine

David, R. (2013, December 13). *L'aide-soignante de Chambéry était traumatisée par la mort de sa mère*. Le Figaro.
https://www.lefigaro.fr/actualite-france/2013/12/13/01016-20131213ARTFIG00513-l-aide-soignante-de-chambery-seule-et-traumatisee-par-la-mort-de-sa-mere.php

Dostoyevsky, F. (2022). *Crime and punishment*. Chartwell Books.

Edmond J Cullen. (n.d.). Ancestry.com.
https://www.ancestry.com/genealogy/records/edmond-j-cullen-24-81xg3w

Estephe, S. (n.d.). *Unknown gender history*. Blogspot.com.
https://unknownmisandry.blogspot.com/2018/12/ludivine-chambet-serial-killer-nurse.html

Goad, J. (2020, January 14). *KILLER NURSES: 20 caregivers who murdered their patients*. Thought Catalog.
https://thoughtcatalog.com/jim-goad/2020/01/killer-nurses-20-caregivers-who-murdered-their-patients/

Greiss, L. (2022, October 31). Cedar Crest College criticizes use of diploma in 'The Good Nurse,' movie about killer nurse Charles Cullen. *Morning Call*.
https://www.mcall.com/2022/10/31/cedar-crest-college-criticizes-use-of-diploma-in-the-good-nurse-movie-about-killer-nurse-charles-cullen/

Grine, J. D., Smith, D. K., & Lersch, T. (n.d.). *Digital commons @ UnivDigital commons @ university of ersity of south Florida south Florida*. Usf.edu. https://digitalcommons.usf.edu/cgi/viewcontent.cgi?article=2379&context=etd

Halliday, J. (2023, June 20). Lucy Letby 'playing God' when she attacked and killed babies, court hears. *The Guardian*. https://www.theguardian.com/uk-news/2023/jun/20/lucy-letby-playing-god-when-she-attacked-killed-babies-court-hears

Halliday, J., Blight, G., Kirk, A., & Fischer, H. (2023, August 18). Timeline of Lucy Letby's attacks on babies and when alarm was raised. *The Guardian*. https://www.theguardian.com/uk-news/ng-interactive/2023/aug/18/lucy-letby-timeline-attacks-babies-when-alarm-raised

Harding, L. (2006, February 8). German nurse accused of killing 29 patients. *The Guardian*. https://www.theguardian.com/world/2006/feb/08/germany.lukeharding

Harold Shipman. (2014, April 2). Biography. https://www.biography.com/crime/harold-shipman

Home, L. R. P. F., & Cremation Service. (n.d.). *Obituary for Anna Bell Majors*. https://www.lrpetty.com/notices/Anna-Majors

Jackson, T., & Smith, R. (2004). Harold Shipman. *BMJ : British Medical Journal, 328*(7433), 231.

Jenkins, J. P. (2023). Harold Shipman. In *Encyclopedia Britannica*.

Kugler, D. (2021, September 3). *Charles Cullen: New Jersey's angel of death*. Https://the-line-up.com; Open Road Media. https://the-line-up.com/charles-cullen

Kuperinsky, A. (2022, October 26). *Meet 'The Good Nurse' hero who helped put N.J. serial killer Charles Cullen behind bars*. Nj.

https://www.nj.com/entertainment/2022/10/meet-the-good-nurse-hero-who-helped-put-nj-serial-killer-charles-cullen-behind-bars.html

Logan, S. (2021, March 4). *The Marymount hospital "serial killer."* Kentucky Historic Institutions. https://kyhi.org/2021/03/04/the-marymount-hospital-serial-killer/

Ludivine Chambet. (n.d.). Vice.com. https://www.vice.com/en/topic/ludivine-chambet

Ludivine Chambet: Nursing assistant to poisoner. (2021, January 28). Grave Reviews. https://gravereviews.com/2021/01/28/ludivine-chambet-nursing-assistant-to-poisoner/

Media, H. (2014, August 27). *Nurse dubbed the "angel of death" said he was helping patients by killing them.* Medical Bag. https://www.medicalbag.com/home/specialties/nurse-practitioners/nurse-dubbed-the-angel-of-death-said-he-was-helping-patients-by-killing-them/

Moreau, C. (2022, October 14). *Full list: the deaths and collapses Lucy Letby is accused of causing.* Hereford Times. https://www.herefordtimes.com/news/23049595.full-list-deaths-collapses-lucy-letby-accused-causing/

NexDev. (2017, May 24). *Euthanasia: Nursing assistant receives 25-year prison term.* AllianceVITA. https://www.alliancevita.org/en/2017/05/euthanasia-nursing-assistant-receives-25-year-prison-term/

Olson, S. (2022a, September 28). *"The Good Nurse": A complete timeline of Charles Cullen's victims.* Seventeen. https://www.seventeen.com/celebrity/movies-tv/a41793010/the-good-nurse-charles-cullen-victims-timeline/

Olson, S. (2022b, September 28). *"The Good Nurse": A complete timeline of Charles Cullen's victims.* Seventeen.

https://www.seventeen.com/celebrity/movies-tv/a41793010/the-good-nurse-charles-cullen-victims-timeline/

Parisien, L. (2016, December 7). Empoisonneuse de Chambéry : Ludivine Chambet, la femme qui ne s'aimait pas. *Le Parisien*. https://www.leparisien.fr/faits-divers/ludivine-chambet-la-femme-qui-ne-s-aimait-pas-07-12-2016-6422541.php

Peach, N. (n.d.). *Here's everything to know about Lucy Letby's parents and family background*. Grazia. https://graziadaily.co.uk/life/in-the-news/lucy-letby-parents-friends/

Potts, M. (2015). *Jane toppan: A Greed, Power, and lust serial killer*. https://www.academia.edu/15686136

Rafford, C. (2022, September 28). The story of Indiana's "Angel of Death," Orville Lynn Majors. *The Indianapolis Star*. https://www.indystar.com/story/news/history/retroindy/2022/09/28/orville-lynn-majors-indianas-angel-of-death-convicted-murdering-patients/69514226007/

Ro Gee 1. (n.d.). SoundCloud. https://soundcloud.com/ro-gee

Seckel, H. (2017, May 19). Au procès de « l'empoisonneuse de Chambéry », un effroyable jeudi. *Le Monde*. https://www.lemonde.fr/police-justice/article/2017/05/19/au-proces-de-l-empoisonneuse-de-chambery-un-effroyable-jeudi_5130343_1653578.html

Serial Killers. (n.d.). *Serial killer Stephan LETTER - the angel of death*. Serialkillercalendar.com. https://www.serialkillercalendar.com/Stephan%20LETTER.php

Shakespeare, W., & Sexton, A. (2008). *Shakespeare's Hamlet*. John Wiley & Sons.

Signs of a sociopath. (n.d.). WebMD. https://www.webmd.com/mental-health/signs-sociopath

Smith, B. H. (2019, July 8). *'angel of death' may have given lethal injections to more than 130 as A nurse*. Oxygen. https://www.oxygen.com/license-to-kill/crime-time/angel-of-death-orville-majors-nurse

Smith, C. R. B. (2015). *Outlaw women: America's most notorious daughters, wives, and mothers*. Rowman & Littlefield.

Stack, L. (2017, March 31). Donald Harvey, who killed dozens of hospital patients, dies at 64. *The New York Times*. https://www.nytimes.com/2017/03/30/us/donald-harvey-who-killed-dozens-of-hospital-patients-dies.html

Swiss nurse admits killing 24. (2004, January 14). UPI. https://www.upi.com/Top_News/2004/01/14/Swiss-nurse-admits-killing-24/63121074110777/

The Editors of Encyclopedia Britannica. (2023). Hippocratic oath. In *Encyclopedia Britannica*.

Tresniowski, A. (1999, November 8). *Death Angel*. PEOPLE. https://people.com/archive/death-angel-vol-52-no-18/

Tuffs, A. (2004). Doctors call for more postmortems after murders at German hospital. *BMJ : British Medical Journal*, *329*(7463), 418.3. https://doi.org/10.1136/bmj.329.7463.418-b

Vadala, N. (2022, October 27). The true story of Charles Cullen, serial killer portrayed in Netflix's 'The Good Nurse.' *Philadelphia Inquirer (Philadelphia, Pa. : 1969)*. https://www.inquirer.com/news/good-nurse-netflix-charles-cullen-20221027.html

Who is Lucy Letby? The nurse who became Britain's most prolific child killer. (n.d.). *Times (London, England: 1788)*. https://www.thetimes.co.uk/article/who-is-lucy-letby-nurse-killed-family-babies-background-family-friends-education-s7njrswmc

(N.d.-a). Afa.org. https://secure.afa.org/Mitchell/reports/1204vietnam.pdf

(N.d.-b). Com.au. https://www.heraldsun.com.au/news/law-order/angels-of-death-tells-how-nurse-charles-cullen-killed-patients/news-story/3f1482705c3ee2a6ff47238fdb1f0fa6

(N.d.-c). Com.au. https://www.heraldsun.com.au/news/law-order/angels-of-death-tells-how-nurse-charles-cullen-killed-patients/news-story/3f1482705c3ee2a6ff47238fdb1f0fa6#:~:text=A%20few%20weeks%20after%20he,Ms%20Tomlinson%20out%20to%20dinner.

Made in the USA
Monee, IL
27 March 2025

14766029R00085